ロングマン

英和フォト・ディクショナリー

LONGMAN ENGLISH-JAPANESE PHOTO DICTIONARY

Marilyn S. Rosenthal and Daniel B. Freeman

Longman

INTRODUCTION　まえがき

「ロングマン英和フォト・ディクショナリー」は、北米の生活と言語を写真を使って詳細に紹介しています。語彙と会話の練習書として、2000語以上を80以上の語義カテゴリーで収録しました。現代アメリカ文化をカラー写真で、文脈的（The Dining Room）にあるいは分類的（Emotions）に学習できます。

「ロングマン英和フォト・ディクショナリー」はまた、アルファベット順の配列、連想ゲーム、ヒヤリング練習、ディクテーション、物語創作、カテゴリー化、ライティング練習、作文、討論、議論、ペアを組んであるいはグループによる学習等にもご利用いただけます。各ユニットを学習するたびに「聞く」、「話す」、「読む」、「書く」の４つの能力が身につきます。語学力に合わせて、また必要に応じてご利用ください。

ユニットはそれぞれ独立しており、難易度順にはなっておりません。教える状況に最も適した方法でユニットを選択なさることをお勧めします。例えば、Numbers と Money and Banking を組み合わせたり、各家庭の部屋を Action at Home といっしょに学習することもできます。

本辞典は、言語と文化の基本的参考書として、主要教本または補充教材として様々なレベルでご利用いただくことを目的としております。写真を使用することによって教師も生徒もより深い興味を持ち、その時々の話題が議題となれば幸いです。皆様からのご意見・ご感想等ございましたら、どうぞお知らせください。

Marilyn Rosenthal ╱ Daniel Freeman

CONTENTS 目 次

NUMBERS 数

1 one 一	**11** eleven 十一	**21** twenty-one 二十一	**1,000** one thousand 千
2 two 二	**12** twelve 十二	**30** thirty 三十	**10,000** ten thousand 万
3 three 三	**13** thirteen 十三	**40** forty 四十	**100,000** one hundred thousand 十万
4 four 四	**14** fourteen 十四	**50** fifty 五十	**1,000,000** one million 百万
5 five 五	**15** fifteen 十五	**60** sixty 六十	**+** plus プラス
6 six 六	**16** sixteen 十六	**70** seventy 七十	**−** minus マイナス
7 seven 七	**17** seventeen 十七	**80** eighty 八十	**×** times かける
8 eight 八	**18** eighteen 十八	**90** ninety 九十	**÷** divided by 割る
9 nine 九	**19** nineteen 十九	**100** one hundred 百	**=** equals イコール
10 ten 十	**20** twenty 二十	**101** one hundred and one 百一	

¼	⅓	½	¾	1
one quarter / one fourth 四分の一	one third 三分の一	one half 半分／二分の一	three quarters / three fourths 四分の三	one 一

first 一番目／一着　　second 二番目／二着　　third 三番目／三着　　fourth 四番目／四着

100% one hundred percent 百パーセント

10% ten percent 十パーセント

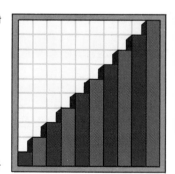

a. clock 時計
b. hour hand 短針
c. minute hand 長針
d. face 文字盤
e. (digital) watch （デジタル）時計
f. (analog) watch （アナログ）時計
g. twelve o'clock / midnight
   12時／夜中の12時
h. twelve o'clock / noon
   12時／正午
i. eight A.M. / eight (o'clock)
   in the morning 午前8時
j. eight P.M. / eight (o'clock)
   at night 午後8時
k. seven o'clock / seven 7時
l. seven o five / five after seven
   7時5分
m. seven ten / ten after seven
   7時10分
n. seven fifteen / a quarter
   after seven 7時15分
o. seven twenty / twenty
   after seven 7時20分
p. seven twenty-five /
   twenty-five after seven
   7時25分
q. seven thirty / half past seven
   7時30分／7時半
r. seven thirty-five / twenty-five
   to eight 7時35分／8時25分前
s. seven forty / twenty to eight
   7時40分／8時20分前
t. seven forty-five / a quarter to
   eight 7時45分／8時15分前
u. seven fifty / ten to eight
   7時50分／8時10分前
v. seven fifty-five / five to eight
   7時55分／8時5分前

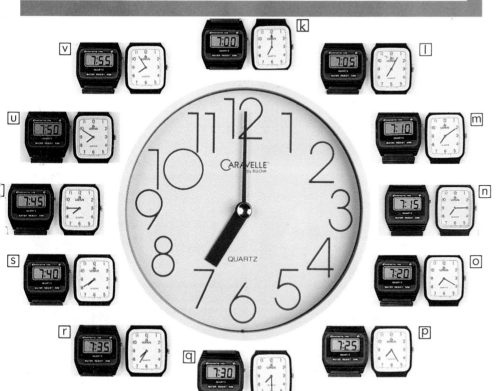

A. Year 年

B. Months 月

January 1月
February 2月
March 3月
April 4月
May 5月
June 6月
July 7月
August 8月
September 9月
October 10月
November 11月
December 12月

C. Days of the Week

S Sunday 日曜日
M Monday 月曜日
T Tuesday 火曜日
W Wednesday 水曜日
T Thursday 木曜日
F Friday 金曜日
S Saturday 土曜日

D. Holidays 祝祭日

1. New Year's Day 元日
2. Valentine's Day
   聖バレンタインデー
3. Washington's Birthday
   ワシントン誕生日
4. St. Patrick's Day
   聖パトリックの日
5. Easter 復活祭
6. Mother's Day 母の日
7. Memorial Day
   戦没将兵記念日
8. Father's Day
   父の日
9. Fourth of July /
   Independence Day
   (in Canada:
   Canada Day, July 1)
   7月4日 / 独立記念日
   [カナダでは：カナダデー、7月1日]
10. Labor Day 労働者の日
11. Halloween ハロウィーン
12. Thanksgiving
    (in Canada: October 10)
    感謝祭 [カナダでは：10月10日]

13. Christmas クリスマス

A 1992

JANUARY

S	M	T	W	T	F	S
		①	1	2	3	4
5	6	7	8	9	10	11
12	13	14	15	16	17	18
19	20	21	22	23	24	25
26	27	28	29	30	31	

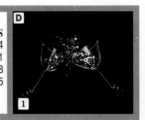

FEBRUARY

S	M	T	W	T	F	S
						1
2	3	4	5	6	7	8
9	10	11	12	13	⑭	15
16	17	18	⑲	20	21	22
23	24	25	26	27	28	29

MARCH

S	M	T	W	T	F	S
1	2	3	4	5	6	7
8	9	10	11	12	13	14
15	16	⑰	18	19	20	21
22	23	24	25	26	27	28
29	30	31				

APRIL

S	M	T	W	T	F	S
			1	2	3	4
5	6	7	8	9	10	11
12	13	14	15	16	17	18
⑲	20	21	22	23	24	25
26	27	28	29	30		

MAY

S	M	T	W	T	F	S
					1	2
3	4	5	6	7	8	9
⑩	11	12	13	14	15	16
17	18	19	20	21	22	23
24	㉕	26	27	28	29	30
31						

JUNE

S	M	T	W	T	F	S
	1	2	3	4	5	6
7	8	9	10	11	12	13
14	15	16	17	18	19	20
㉑	22	23	24	25	26	27
28	29	30				

JULY

S	M	T	W	T	F	S
			1	2	3	④
5	6	7	8	9	10	11
12	13	14	15	16	17	18
19	20	21	22	23	24	25
26	27	28	29	30	31	

AUGUST

S	M	T	W	T	F	S
						1
2	3	4	5	6	7	8
9	10	11	12	13	14	15
16	17	18	19	20	21	22
23	24	25	26	27	28	29
30	31					

No Holiday

SEPTEMBER

S	M	T	W	T	F	S
		1	2	3	4	5
6	⑦	8	9	10	11	12
13	14	15	16	17	18	19
20	21	22	23	24	25	26
27	28	29	30			

OCTOBER

S	M	T	W	T	F	S
				1	2	3
4	5	6	7	8	9	10
11	12	13	14	15	16	17
18	19	20	21	22	23	24
25	26	27	28	29	30	㉛

NOVEMBER

S	M	T	W	T	F	S
1	2	3	4	5	6	7
8	9	10	11	12	13	14
15	16	17	18	19	20	21
22	23	24	25	㉖	27	28
29	30					

DECEMBER

S	M	T	W	T	F	S
		1	2	3	4	5
6	7	8	9	10	11	12
13	14	15	16	17	18	19
20	21	22	23	24	㉕	26
27	28	29	30	31		

WEATHER & SEASONS 天候と季節

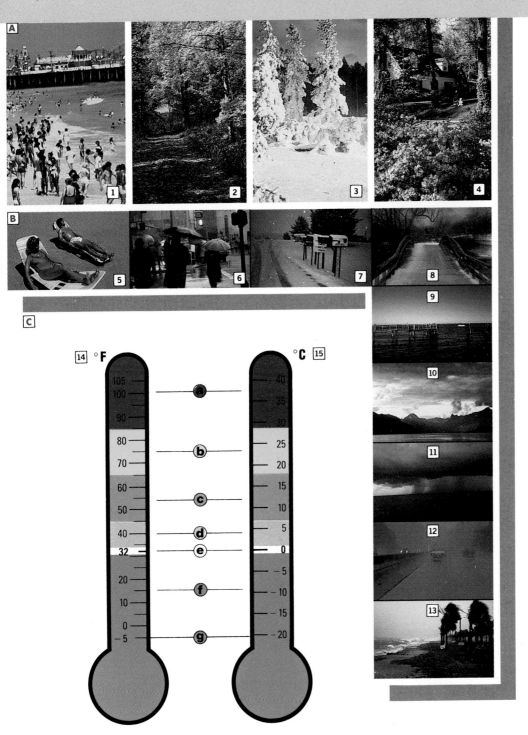

A. Seasons 季節
1. summer 夏
2. fall 秋
3. winter 冬
4. spring 春

B. Weather 天候
5. sunny 晴
6. rainy 雨
7. snowy 雪
8. icy 凍結
9. clear 快晴
10. cloudy 曇り
11. stormy 嵐
12. foggy 霧
13. windy 強風

C. Temperature 気温
14. degrees Fahrenheit 華氏
15. degrees Celsius /
    degrees Centigrade 摂氏
a. hot 暑い
b. warm 暖かい
c. cool / chilly 涼しい/冷える
d. cold 寒い
e. freezing 氷点
f. below freezing 氷点下
g. five(degrees)below
    (zero) / minus twenty
    (degrees)
    華氏零下5度/摂氏マイナス20度

A. Cube 立方体
1. corner 角
2. top 頂面
3. front 前面
4. edge 稜
5. depth 奥行
6. height 高さ

B. Isosceles triangle 二等辺三角形
7. obtuse angle 鈍角
8. acute angle 鋭角

C. Right Triangle 直角三角形
9. apex 頂点
10. hypotenuse 斜辺
11. base 底辺
12. right angle 直角

D. Square 正方形
13. side 辺

E. Rectangle 長方形
14. width 横
15. length 縦
16. diagonal 対角線

F. Circle 円
17. circumference 円周
18. center 中心
19. diameter 直径
20. radius 半径

G. Oval / Ellipse 楕円形

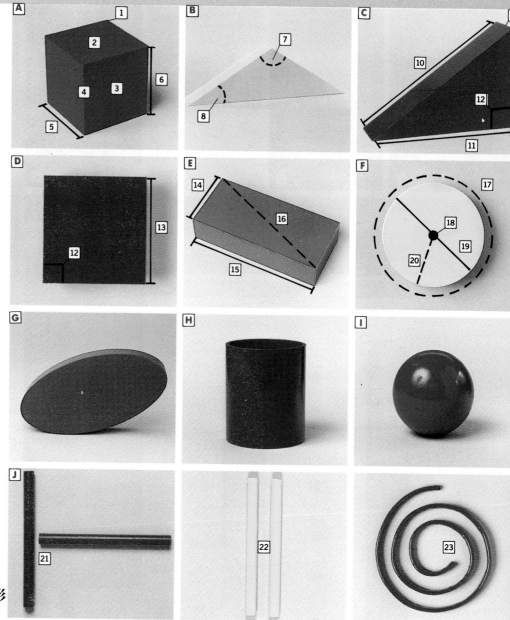

H. Cylinder 円柱

I. Sphere 球

J. Lines 線
21. perpendicular 垂直
22. parallel 平行
23. spiral ら旋

K. Measurements 測定
24. yard stick ヤード尺
25. yard / 0.914 meter
    ヤード / 0.914メートル
26. ruler 定規
27. foot / 0.305 meter
    フィート / 0.305メートル
28. inch / 2.54 centimeters
    インチ / 2.54センチメートル

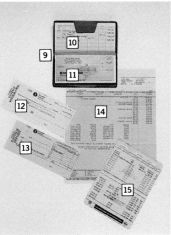
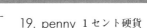

1. teller 出納係
2. customer 客
3. bank officer 銀行員
4. counter カウンター
5. computer コンピューター
6. bank vault 金庫室
7. safe deposit box 貸金庫
8. cash machine / automatic teller 現金自動支払機
9. checkbook 小切手帳
10. check register / record 小切手支払控
11. check 小切手
12. withdrawal slip 預金引出票
13. deposit slip 預金預入票
14. monthly statement 明細書
15. bank book 預金通帳
16. traveler's check トラベラーズ・チェック
17. credit card クレジット・カード
18. money order 為替

19. penny 1セント硬貨
20. nickel 5セント硬貨
21. dime 10セント硬貨
22. quarter 25セント硬貨
23. half dollar / fifty cent piece 50セント硬貨
24. silver dollar 1ドル硬貨
25. dollar (bill) / one dollar 1ドル紙幣
26. five (dollar bill) / five dollars 5ドル紙幣
27. ten (dollar bill) / ten dollars 10ドル紙幣
28. twenty (dollar bill) / twenty dollars 20ドル紙幣
29. fifty (dollar bill) / fifty dollars 50ドル紙幣
30. one hundred (dollar bill) / one hundreddollars 100ドル紙幣

THE WORLD　世界

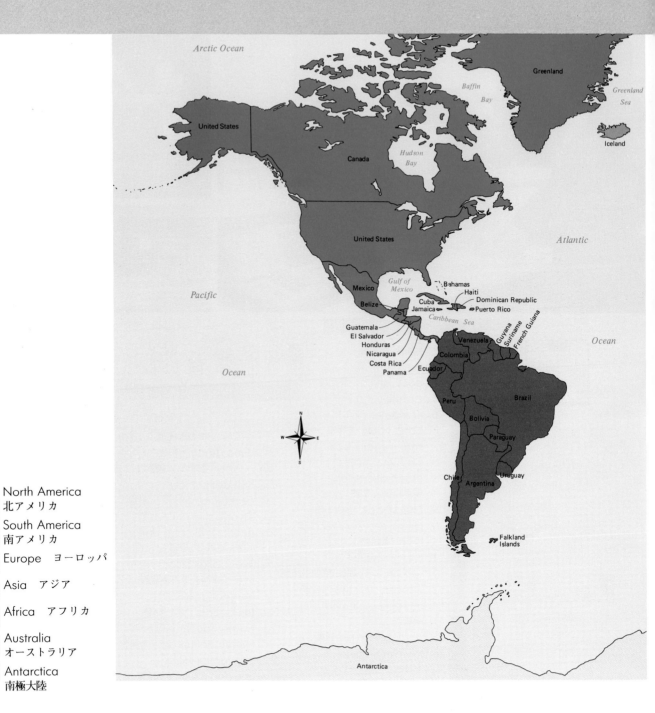

Arctic Ocean

Greenland

Baffin Bay

Greenland Sea

United States

Iceland

Canada

Hudson Bay

United States

Atlantic

Pacific

Mexico

Gulf of Mexico

Bahamas

Haiti

Belize

Cuba

Dominican Republic

Jamaica

Puerto Rico

Caribbean Sea

Ocean

Guatemala

El Salvador

Honduras

Nicaragua

Costa Rica

Panama

Venezuela

Colombia

Ecuador

Guyana

Suriname

French Guiana

Ocean

Peru

Brazil

Bolivia

Paraguay

Chile

Argentina

Uruguay

Falkland Islands

Antarctica

North America
北アメリカ

South America
南アメリカ

Europe　ヨーロッパ

Asia　アジア

Africa　アフリカ

Australia
オーストラリア

Antarctica
南極大陸

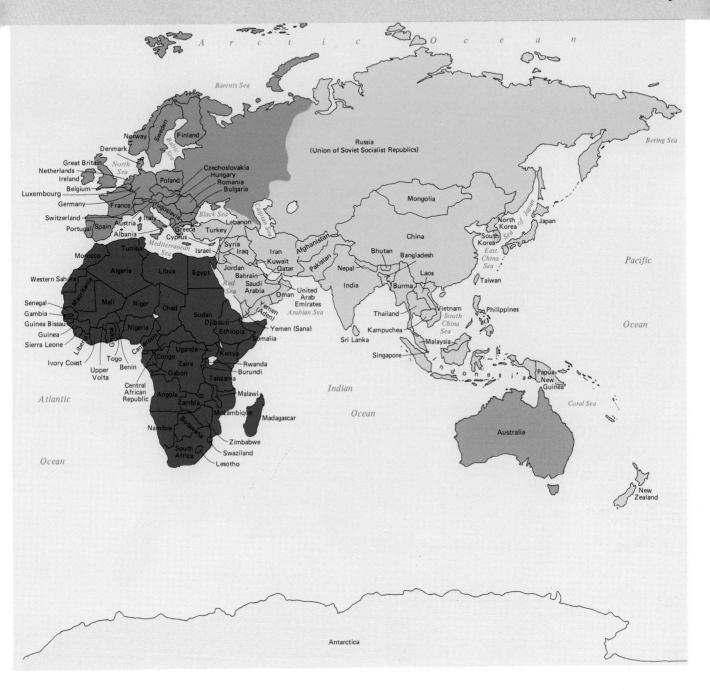

THE UNITED STATES 合衆国

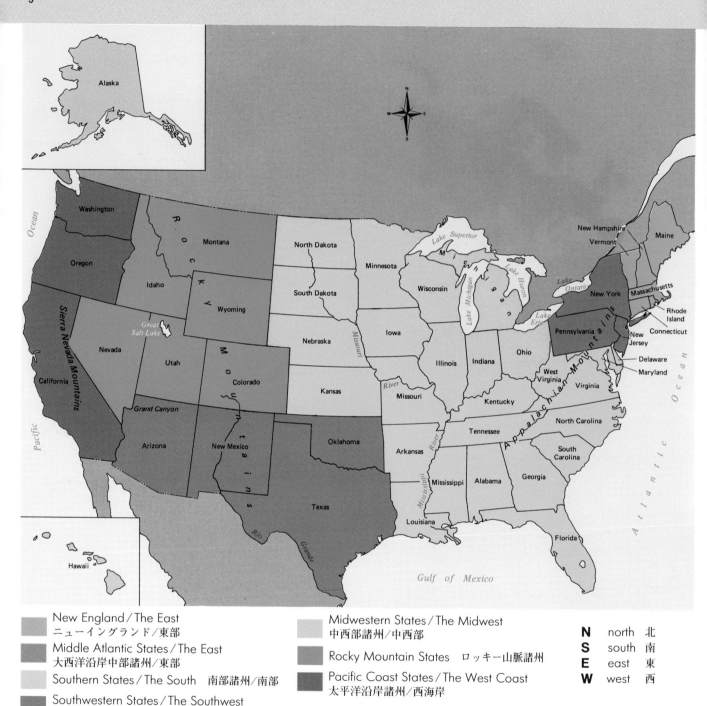

New England / The East
ニューイングランド／東部

Middle Atlantic States / The East
大西洋沿岸中部諸州／東部

Southern States / The South　南部諸州／南部

Southwestern States / The Southwest
南西部諸州／南西部

Midwestern States / The Midwest
中西部諸州／中西部

Rocky Mountain States　ロッキー山脈諸州

Pacific Coast States / The West Coast
太平洋沿岸諸州／西海岸

N north 北
S south 南
E east 東
W west 西

Beaufort
Sea

Queen Elizabeth Islands

Baffin
Bay

Victoria
Island

Baffin
Island

Machenzie Mountains

Northwest Territories

Yukon
Territory

Machenzie River

Labrador
Sea

Hudson
Bay

Newfoundland

Ocean

R o c k y   M o u n t a i n s

British
Columbia

Alberta

Saskatchewan

Manitoba

Quebec

Ocean

Pacific

Ontario

St. Lawrence River

New
Brunswick

Prince
Edward
Island

Nova
Scotia

Atlantic

	Maritime Provinces 沿岸地方		Western Canada 西カナダ
	Quebec ケベック州		Northern Canada 北カナダ
	Ontario オンタリオ州		

THE CITY 都 市

1. skyline スカイライン
2. skyscraper 超高層ビル
3. fire hydrant 消火栓
4. trash can ゴミ箱
5. parking lot 駐車場
6. parking meter
   パーキングメーター
7. traffic light 交通信号
8. flag 旗
9. street 通り
10. crosswalk 横断歩道
11. pedestrian 歩行者
12. bus lane バスレーン
13. (street) corner (通りの) 角
14. curb ふち石
15. phone booth /
    telephone booth
    電話ボックス
16. walk sign 歩行標識
17. one way (traffic) sign
    一方通行標識
18. office building
    オフィスビル

19. traffic (jam)　交通 (渋滞)
20. subway (entrance)
　　地下鉄 (入口)
21. newsstand　新聞売りスタンド
22. street light　街灯
23. bus stop　バス停
24. street sign　街路標識
25. bus　バス
26. exit　出口
27. passenger　乗客
28. sidewalk　歩道

A. Check-out Area
レジ

1. customer / shopper
   客／買物客
2. cashier　レジ係
3. cash register　レジスター
4. checkbook　小切手帳
5. groceries　食料日用雑貨
6. packer　包装係
7. bag / sack　袋
8. check-out counter
   レジ・カウンター

B. Frozen Foods
冷凍食品

9. frozen vegetables
   冷凍野菜
10. frozen dinner　冷凍食
11. frozen orange juice
    冷凍オレンジジュース

C. Dairy　乳製品

12. yogurt　ヨーグルト
13. cheese　チーズ
14. eggs　卵
15. margarine　マーガリン
16. butter　バター
17. milk　牛乳

D. Canned Goods
缶詰食品
18. tuna fish マグロ
19. soup スープ

E. Meat & Poultry
肉製品と鶏肉
20. bacon ベーコン
21. roast ロースト
22. pork chops ポークチョップ
23. chicken / roaster
鶏肉/ロースト用鶏肉
24. ground meat 挽き肉
25. steak ステーキ
26. lamb chops ラムチョップ

F. Packaged Goods
包装食品
27. bread パン
28. cereal シリアル
29. cookies クッキー
30. crackers クラッカー
31. macaroni マカロニ

FRUIT 果物

1. apples りんご
2. pears なし
3. grapes ぶどう
4. kiwis キーウィー
5. mangoes マンゴー
6. coconuts ココナツ
7. avocados アボカド
8. bananas バナナ
9. nectarines
   ネクタリン
10. plums プラム
11. cherries
    さくらんぼ
12. apricots あんず
13. lemons レモン
14. limes ライム
15. grapefruits
    グレープフルーツ
16. oranges オレンジ
17. pineapples
    パイナップル
18. papayas パパイヤ
19. peaches もも
20. strawberries
    いちご
21. raspberries
    ラズベリー
22. blueberries
    ブルーベリー
23. watermelons
    すいか
24. honeydew melons
    ハニデューメロン
25. cantaloupes
    カンタロープメロン

VEGETABLES 野菜

1. lettuce レタス
2. green onions / scallions 葉玉ねぎ
3. radishes ラディッシュ
4. watercress クレソン
5. tomatoes トマト
6. cucumbers きゅうり
7. celery セロリ
8. yellow peppers 黄ピーマン
9. green peppers ピーマン
10. red peppers 赤ピーマン
11. new potatoes 新じゃがいも
12. baking potatoes ベークドポテト用ポテト
13. sweet potatoes さつまいも
14. onions 玉ねぎ
15. red onions 赤玉ねぎ
16. pearl onions 小粒の玉ねぎ

17. cauliflower カリフラワー
18. spinach ほうれん草
19. garlic にんにく
20. artichokes アーティチョーク
21. green beans / string beans いんげん豆
22. eggplants なす
23. carrots にんじん
24. asparagus アスパラガス
25. broccoli ブロッコリー
26. corn とうもろこし
27. ginger しょうが
28. parsnips パースニップ
29. cabbage キャベツ
30. leeks リーキ/西洋ねぎ
31. turnips かぶ
32. dill イノンド

THE MENU メニュー

A. Appetizers 前菜/オードブル

1. tomato juice トマトジュース
2. fruit cup / fruit cocktail フルーツカクテル
3. shrimp cocktail えびのカクテル

B. Soup and Salad スープとサラダ

4. soup スープ
5. (tossed) salad （トスト）サラダ

C. Main Courses / Entrees 主菜

6. steak ステーキ
7. baked potatoes ベークドポテト
8. (dinner) roll （ディナー用）ロールパン
9. roast beef ローストビーフ
10. stuffed tomatoes トマトの詰物
11. pork chops ポークチョップ
12. sweet potatoes さつまいも
13. spaghetti and meatballs スパゲティー・ミートボール
14. roast chicken ローストチキン
15. green beans いんげん豆
16. peaches もも
17. fish 魚
18. broccoli ブロッコリー

D. Desserts デザート

19. apple pie アップルパイ
20. chocolate cake チョコレートケーキ
21. ice cream アイスクリーム
22. jello ゼリー

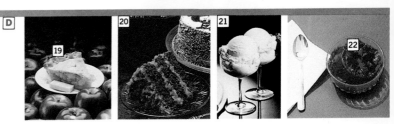

E. Beverages 飲物

23. coffee コーヒー
24. tea 紅茶

1. hero / submarine sandwich
   サブマリン・サンドイッチ
2. roast beef sandwich
   ローストビーフ・サンドイッチ
3. pizza ピザ
4. fried clams
   はまぐり・あさりのフライ
5. fried chicken
   フライドチキン
6. mustard からし
7. ketchup ケチャップ
8. relish 付合わせ
9. pickles ピクルス
10. onions 玉ねぎ
11. potato chips
    ポテトチップス
12. tortilla chips
    トルティヤチップス
13. pretzels プレッツェル
14. popcorn ポップコーン
15. peanuts ピーナッツ
16. candy bar / chocolate
    キャンディーバー／
    チョコレート
17. (chewing) gum
    (チューイング) ガム
18. donut ドーナツ
19. milk shake ミルクセーキ
20. soft drink / soda
    ソフト・ドリンク／炭酸飲料
21. straw ストロー
22. (paper) napkin
    (紙) ナプキン
23. (paper) plate (紙) 皿
24. hamburger ハンバーガー
25. hot dog ホットドッグ
26. onion rings オニオンリング
27. french fries
    ポテトフライ

THE POST OFFICE 郵便局

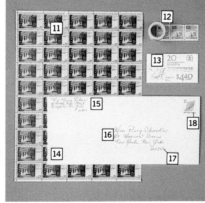

1. postal clerk
   郵便局員
2. package / parcel
   小包
3. scale はかり
4. express mail
   速達便
5. mail slot
   郵便物投函口
6. mail truck 郵便車
7. mail carrier
   郵便配達人
8. mailbag 郵便袋
9. mailbox 郵便箱
10. stamp machine
    切手販売機
11. sheet of stamps
    切手シート
12. roll of stamps
    切手ロール
13. book of stamps
    切手冊子／つづり
14. envelope 封筒
15. return address
    差出人住所
16. address 住所
17. zip code 郵便番号
18. stamp 切手
19. (picture) postcard
    (絵) 葉書
20. return receipt
    配達証明書
21. certified mail
    書留郵便

THE OFFICE オフィス

1. secretary 秘書
2. (desk) lamp 電気スタンド
3. index file / Rolodex
   インデックス
4. pencil holder 鉛筆立て
5. (electric) pencil
   sharpener (電動) 鉛筆削り
6. typewriter タイプライター
7. typing paper タイプ用紙
8. tape dispenser
   セロテープ台
9. tape / scotch tape
   テープ／セロテープ
10. stapler ホッチキス
11. in box 書類受 (入)
12. out box 書類受 (出)
13. paper clip holder
    クリップ入れ
14. stationery 便せん
15. wastepaper basket
    くずかご
16. file cabinet
    ファイルキャビネット
17. file folder
    ファイルフォルダー
18. bulletin board
    掲示板／ボード
19. receptionist 受付係
20. telephone / switchboard
    電話／交換機
21. note pad メモ帳
22. message pad
    メッセージ用紙
23. desk calendar
    卓上カレンダー
24. desk 机
25. (ball point) pen
    ボールペン
26. pencil 鉛筆
27. eraser 消しゴム
28. rubber band 輪ゴム
29. paper clip
    クリップ
30. staple ホッチキスの針
31. photocopier / Xerox
    machine コピー機

1. construction worker
建設作業員
2. bricklayer / mason
れんが職人
3. carpenter 大工
4. painter ペンキ屋
5. window washer
窓清掃員
6. sanitation worker
ゴミ収集員
7. truck driver
トラック運転手
8. mechanic 機械修理工
9. welder 溶接工
10. electrician 電気工
11. plumber 配管工
12. firefighter 消防士
13. police officer 警察官
14. letter carrier
郵便配達人
15. fisherman 漁師
16. farmer 農夫
17. florist 花屋
18. grocer 食料品店
19. butcher 肉屋
20. baker パン屋
21. chef / cook
シェフ / コック
22. waiter ウェーター
23. waitress ウェートレス

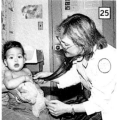
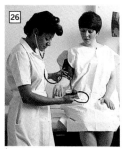
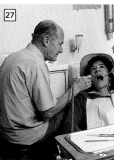

24. scientist 科学者
25. doctor / pediatrician
    医者/小児科医
26. nurse 看護婦
27. dentist 歯科医
28. (dental) hygienist
    歯科衛生士
29. optometrist 検眼士
30. veterinarian 獣医
31. pharmacist 薬剤士
32. newscaster
    ニュース・キャスター
33. journalist
    ジャーナリスト
34. computer technician
    コンピューター技師
35. teacher 教師
36. architect 建築家
37. secretary 秘書
38. teller 出納係
39. salesperson 販売員
40. hairdresser 美容師
41. barber 理容師
42. tailor 仕立て屋
43. seamstress 縫い子
44. model モデル
45. photographer 写真家
46. artist 画家

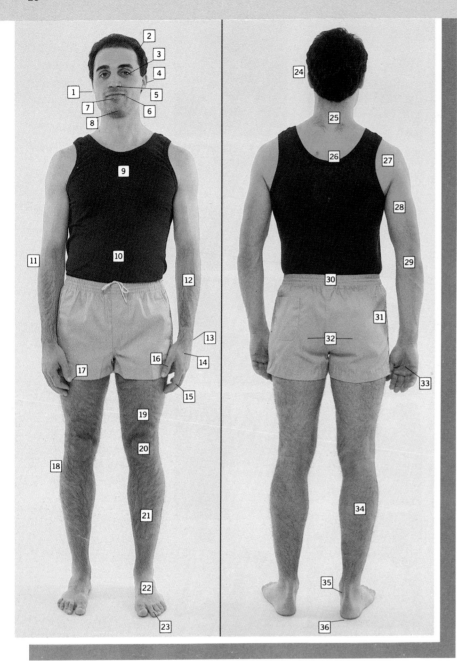

1. face 顔
2. hair 髪
3. eye 目
4. ear 耳
5. nose 鼻
6. mouth 口
7. lip 唇
8. chin あご
9. chest 胸
10. stomach 腹
11. arm 腕
12. forearm 前腕
13. wrist 手首
14. hand 手
15. finger 指
16. thumb 親指
17. nail 爪
18. leg 脚
19. thigh 太もも
20. knee ひざ
21. shin すね
22. foot 足
23. toe つま先
24. head 頭
25. neck 首
26. back 背中
27. shoulder 肩
28. upper arm 上腕
29. elbow ひじ
30. waist ウエスト
31. hip 腰まわり
32. buttocks 尻
33. palm 手のひら
34. calf ふくらはぎ
35. ankle 足首
36. heel かかと

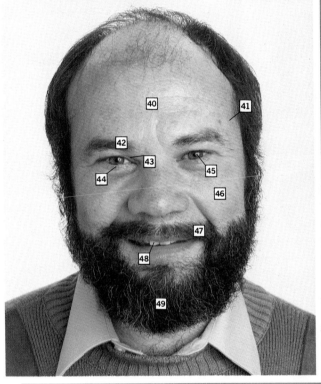

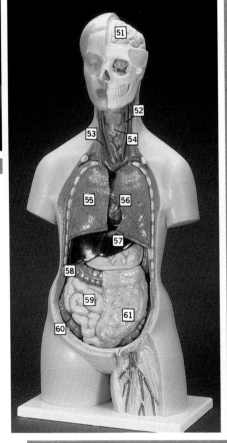

37. blonde 金髪
38. brunette ブルーネット
39. redhead 赤毛
40. forehead ひたい
41. temple こめかみ
42. eyebrow まゆ毛
43. eyelid まぶた
44. eyelash まつ毛
45. pupil ひとみ
46. cheek ほお
47. mustache 口ひげ
48. tooth 歯
49. beard あごひげ
50. tongue 舌

51. brain 脳
52. artery 動脈
53. vein 静脈
54. throat のど
55. lung 肺
56. heart 心臓
57. liver 肝臓
58. gall bladder 胆のう
59. small intestine 小腸
60. large intestine 大腸
61. fatty tissue 脂肪組織

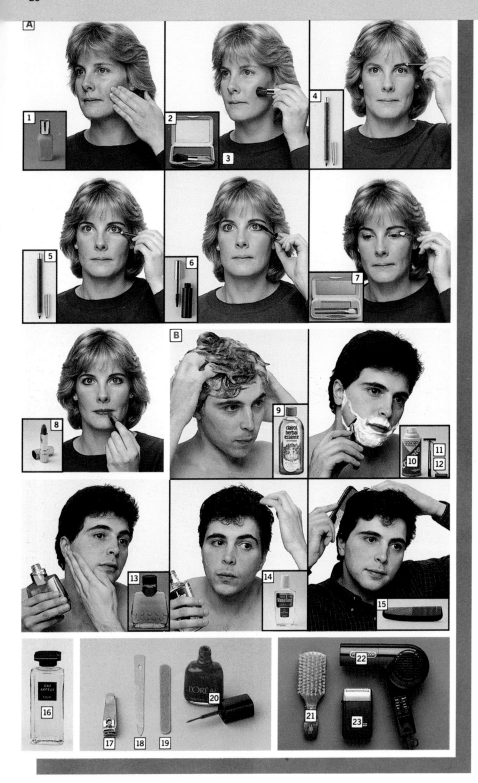

A. Cosmetics 化粧品

1. base / foundation
   ファンデーション
2. blush / rouge ほお紅
3. brush ブラシ
4. eyebrow pencil まゆ墨
5. eyeliner アイライナー
6. mascara マスカラ
7. eye shadow アイシャドー
8. lipstick 口紅

B. Toiletries 洗面用品

9. shampoo シャンプー
10. shaving cream
    シェービング・クリーム
11. razor かみそり
12. razor blade かみそりの刃
13. after-shave (lotion)
    アフターシェーブ(ローション)
14. hair tonic ヘアトニック
15. comb くし
16. cologne コロン
17. nail clipper 爪切り
18. nail file 爪やすり
19. emery board 爪やすり
20. nail polish マニキュア
21. (hair) brush ヘアブラシ
22. hair dryer ヘアドライヤー
23. electric shaver 電気かみそり

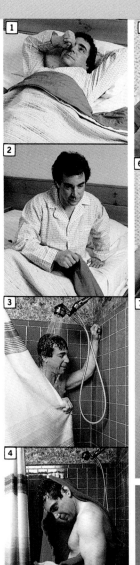

5. brush your teeth
歯を磨く
6. shave
ひげをそる
7. get dressed
服を着る

1. wake up
目覚める
2. get up 起きる
3. take a shower
シャワーに入る
4. dry off 拭く

8. wash your face
顔を洗う
9. rinse your face
顔をすすぐ
10. put on makeup
化粧する
11. brush your hair
髪にブラシをかける

12. cook 料理する
13. eat 食べる
14. drink 飲む
15. sweep 掃く
16. dust ほこりを取る
17. watch (TV)
(テレビを) 見る
18. listen 聞く

19. take a bath
風呂に入る
20. comb your hair
髪をとかす
21. go to bed
寝る
22. sleep 眠る

ACTION AT THE GYM　ジムでの活動

1. bend　曲げる
2. stretch　伸びをする
3. sit　座る
4. lie down　横になる

5. kneel　ひざまづく
6. walk　歩く
7. hop　片足跳び
8. run　走る

9. swing　体を振る
10. reach　届く
11. catch　受ける
12. throw　投げる

13. push　押す
14. lift　持ち上げる
15. pull　引く
16. kick　ける

ACTION AT SCHOOL 学校活動

1. write　書く
2. teach　教える
3. erase　消す
4. give　上げる
5. take　もらう
6. tear up　破る
7. carry　運ぶ
8. read　読む
9. pick up　拾う
10. paint
　　絵の具で描く
11. sculpt
　　彫刻する
12. cut　切る

13. draw　描く
14. smile　ほほえむ
15. laugh　笑う
16. point　指でさす
17. touch　触れる
18. frown
　　顔をしかめる
19. go up　昇る
20. wave
　　手をふる
21. stand　立つ
22. go down
　　降りる
23. fall　落ちる

THE DOCTOR 医師

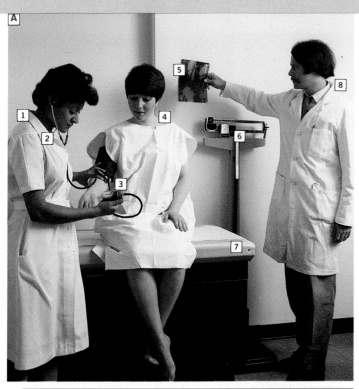

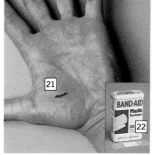
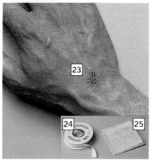

A. The Doctor's Office 診療室

1. nurse 看護婦
2. stethoscope 聴診器
3. blood pressure gauge 血圧計
4. patient 患者
5. x-ray レントゲン
6. scale はかり
7. examination table 診察台
8. doctor 医師

B. Sickness and Medicine 病気と薬

9. headache 頭痛
10. aspirin アスピリン
11. fever 熱
12. thermometer 体温計
13. cold 風邪
14. tissue / Kleenex ティッシュ／クリネックス
15. cold tablets 風邪薬
16. cough 咳
17. cough syrup 咳止めシロップ
18. cough drops 咳止めドロップ
19. stomachache 腹痛
20. antacid / Alka Seltzer 制酸剤／アルカ・セルツァー
21. cut 切り傷
22. Band-Aid バンドエイド
23. scratch ひっかき傷
24. adhesive tape 粘着テープ
25. bandage / gauze 包帯／ガーゼ
26. prescription 処方箋

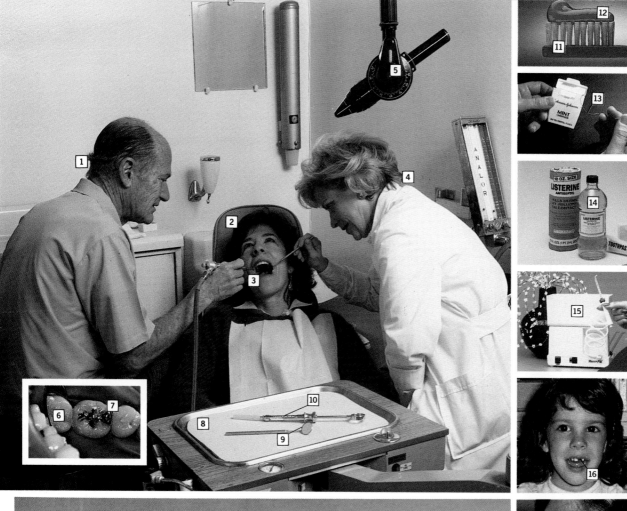

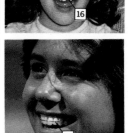

1. dentist　歯科医
2. patient　患者
3. drill　ドリル
4. dental assistant
   歯科助手
5. x-ray machine
   レントゲン撮影器
6. tooth　歯

7. filling　つめ物
8. tray　盆
9. mirror　鏡
10. Novocain　ノボカイン
    （局所麻酔剤）
11. toothbrush　歯ブラシ
12. toothpaste　練り歯磨き

13. dental floss
    デンタル・フロス
14. mouthwash　うがい薬
15. Water Pik
    ウォーター・ピック
    （歯間洗浄器）
16. missing tooth　歯抜け
17. overbite　過蓋咬合
18. braces　矯正器

THE KENNEDY FAMILY　ケネディ家

husband and wife **A** & **B**　夫と妻
father and son **A** & **C**　父と息子
father and daughter **A** & **E**　父と娘
mother and son **B** & **C**　母と息子
mother and daughter **B** & **E**　母と娘
brother and sister **C** & **E**　兄と妹
brothers **C** & **G**　兄弟
sisters **M** & **O**　姉妹
brother-in-law and sister-in-law **C** & **H**
　義理の兄と義理の妹
brothers-in-law **C** & **F**　義理の兄弟
sisters-in-law **E** & **H**　義理の姉妹
father-in-law and son-in-law **A** & **F**
　義理の父と義理の息子
father-in-law and daughter-in-law **A** & **H**
　義理の父と義理の娘

mother-in-law and son-in-law **B** & **F**
　義理の母と義理の息子
mother-in-law and daughter-in-law **B** & **H**
　義理の母と義理の娘
parents and children **A** **B** & **C** **E** **G**　両親と子供
grandparents and grandchildren **A** **B** & **I**　祖父母と孫
grandfather and grandson **A** & **J**　祖父と孫息子
grandfather and granddaughter **A** & **I**　祖父と孫娘
grandmother and grandson **B** & **J**　祖母と孫息子
grandmother and granddaughter **B** & **I**　祖母と孫娘
uncle and nephew **C** & **K**　叔父と甥
uncle and niece **C** & **L**　叔父と姪
aunt and nephew **D** & **K**　叔母と甥
aunt and niece **D** & **L**　叔母と姪
cousins **I** **J** & **K** **L** & **M** **N** **O**　いとこ

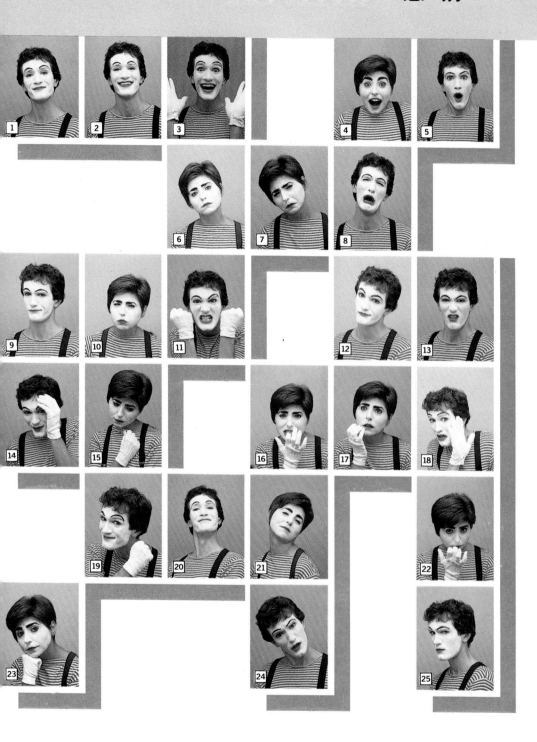

1. pleased　満足した
2. happy　幸わせな
3. ecstatic　有頂天な
4. surprised　驚いた
5. shocked　ぎょっとした
6. sad　悲しい
7. miserable　みじめな
8. grieving　悲嘆にくれた
9. displeased　不満な
10. angry / mad　怒った
11. furious　激怒した
12. annoyed　不愉快な
13. disgusted　うんざりした
14. embarrassed
　　当惑した
15. ashamed　恥ずかしい
16. nervous　神経質な
17. worried　心配した
18. scared / afraid　恐れて
19. determined
　　決心の固い
20. proud　誇り高い
21. smug　気どった
22. shy　内気な
23. bored　退屈した
24. confused　混乱した
25. suspicious　疑い深い

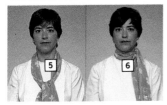

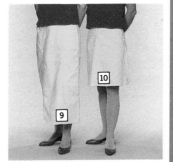

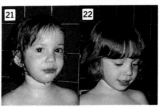

1. neat
   整とんされた
2. messy 乱雑な

3. high 高い
4. low 低い

5. loose ゆるい
6. tight きつい

7. light 軽い
8. heavy 重い

9. long 長い
10. short 短かい

11. good 良い
12. bad 悪い

13. tall 背が高い
14. short 背が低い

15. young 若い
16. old 年とった

17. clean きれいな
18. dirty きたない

19. pretty 美人の
20. ugly 醜い

21. wet ぬれた
22. dry 乾いた

23. straight
    まっすぐな
24. curly 巻き毛の

25. fast 速い
26. slow 遅い

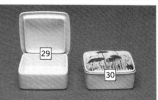

27. hot 熱い
28. cold 冷たい

29. open 開いた
30. closed 閉じた

31. full いっぱい
32. empty からの

33. new 新しい
34. old 古い

35. light 明かるい
36. dark 暗い

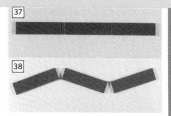

37. straight まっすぐ
38. crooked 曲った

39. wide 広い
40. narrow 狭い

41. thick 太い
42. thin 細い

43. soft やわらかい
44. hard かたい

45. smooth なめらかな
46. rough ざらざらした

47. over 上
48. under 下

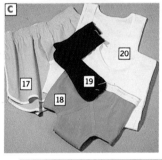

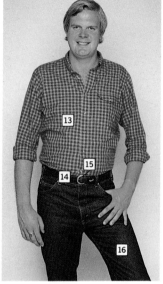

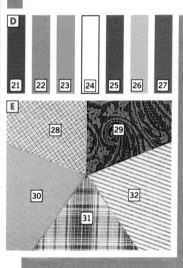

A. The Suit　背広

1. suit　背広
2. jacket　ジャケット
3. sleeve　袖
4. lapel　下えり
5. shirt　ワイシャツ
6. collar　えり
7. tie　ネクタイ
8. vest　チョッキ

B. Casual Wear
カジュアルウェア

9. sport jacket / sport coat

　　スポーツ ジャケット
10. pocket　ポケット
11. sweater　セーター
12. slacks / pants　ズボン
13. sport shirt
　　スポーツシャツ
14. belt　ベルト
15. (belt) buckle
　　(ベルト) バックル
16. jeans　ジーンズ

C. Underwear
下着

17. boxer shorts
　　トランクス
18. briefs / Jockey shorts
　　ブリーフ
19. sock　ソックス
20. undershirt / t-shirt
　　シャツ / T-シャツ

D. Colors　色

21. brown　茶
22. gray　グレー
23. green　緑
24. white　白
25. red　赤
26. tan　黄褐色
27. blue　青

E. Patterns
模様

28. checked　チェック
29. paisley　ペーズリー
30. solid　無地
31. plaid　格子
32. striped　しま

WOMEN'S WEAR 婦人服

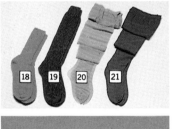

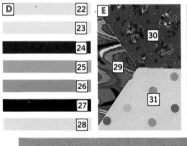

A. The Suit and Dress
スーツとドレス

1. suit スーツ
2. jacket ジャケット
3. skirt スカート
4. blouse ブラウス
5. handbag ハンドバッグ
6. dress ワンピース
7. clutch bag
   セカンドバッグ

B. Casual Wear
カジュアルウェア

8. blazer ブレザー
9. slacks / pants
   スラックス／ズボン
10. shoulder bag
    ショルダーバッグ
11. sweatshirt トレーナー
12. jeans ジーンズ
13. t-shirt T-シャツ
14. shorts 半ズボン／短パン

C. Underwear
下着

15. (half) slip
    スリップ／ペチコート
16. bra ブラジャー
17. underpants / panties
    パンティー
18. sock ソックス
19. knee sock
    ハイソックス
20. panty hose
    パンティーストッキング
21. tights タイツ

D. Colors 色

22. pink ピンク
23. yellow 黄色
24. purple 紫色
25. orange seller だいだ
    い色／オレンジ色
26. turquoise 青みどり
27. black 黒
28. beige ベージュ

E. Patterns
模様

29. print プリント
30. flowered 花柄
31. polka dot 水玉

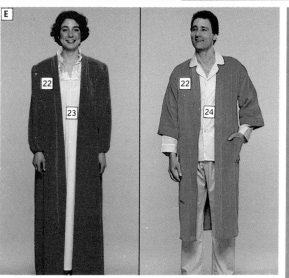

A. Outerwear
外出着
1. coat コート
2. jacket ジャケット
3. cap （縁なし）帽子
4. hat 帽子
5. glove 手袋

B. Rainwear
雨具類
6. umbrella 傘
7. raincoat / trench coat
   レインコート/トレンチコート
8. rain hat レインハット

C. Sweaters
セーター
9. crewneck 丸首
10. turtleneck
    タートルネック
11. V-neck Vネック
12. cardigan カーデガン

D. Footwear
はきもの
13. shoe 靴
14. heel かかと
15. sole 靴底
16. shoelace 靴ひも
17. loafer ローファー
18. sneaker スニーカー
19. sandal サンダル
20. slipper スリッパ
21. boot ブーツ

E. Nightwear
寝間着
22. robe ガウン
23. nightgown ネグリジェ
24. pajamas パジャマ

ACCESSORIES アクセサリー

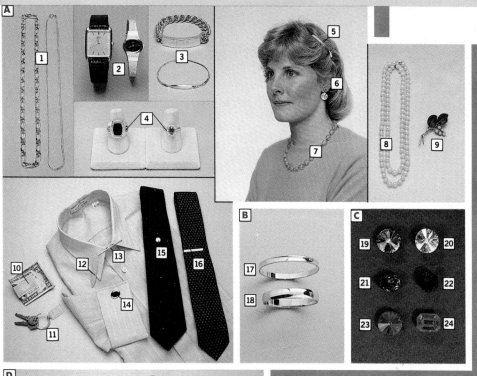

A. Jewelry 宝石装身類

1. chain チェーンネックレス
2. watch 腕時計
3. bracelet ブレスレット
4. ring 指輪
5. barrette ヘアクリップ
6. earring イアリング
7. necklace ネックレス
8. pearls 真珠
9. pin ブローチ
10. money clip 紙幣クリップ
11. key ring キーホルダー
12. stay ステー
13. collar bar カラーバー
14. cuff link カフスボタン
15. tiepin / tie tack
    タイピン/タイタック
16. tie bar / tie clip タイクリップ

B. Metals 貴金属製品

17. gold 金
18. silver 銀

C. Gems 宝石

19. topaz トパーズ
20. diamond ダイヤモンド
21. amethyst アメジスト
22. ruby ルビー
23. sapphire サファイア
24. emerald エメラルド

D. Accessories 小物・グッズ類

25. briefcase ブリーフケース
26. tote bag 手さげバッグ
27. attaché case アタッシュケース
28. change purse 小銭入れ
29. wallet さいふ
30. scarf スカーフ
31. handkerchief ハンカチ

HOUSING 住宅

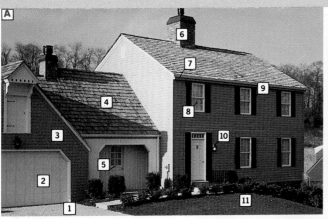

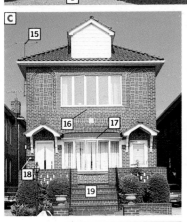

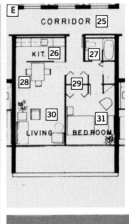

A. Two-Story House 二階建の家

1. driveway ドライブウェイ
2. garage door ガレージ ドア
3. garage ガレージ
4. roof 屋根
5. side door 勝手口
6. chimney 煙突
7. gutter とい
8. window 窓
9. shutter シャッター
10. (porch) light (ポーチ) ライト
11. lawn 芝生

B. Ranch House 平屋

12. front walk
   (門から入口までの) 歩道
13. doorknob ドアノブ
14. front door 玄関のドア

C. Two-Family House / Duplex
二戸一／二世帯住宅

15. antenna アンテナ
16. upstairs apartment
   階上のアパート
17. downstairs apartment
   階下のアパート
18. mailbox 郵便受け
19. (front) steps 正面階段

D. Apartment Building アパート

20. lobby ロビー
21. elevator エレベーター
22. first floor 一階
23. second floor 二階
24. balcony バルコニー

E. Floor Plan 間取図

25. hall / corridor 廊下
26. kitchen 台所
27. bathroom 浴室
28. dining room 食堂
29. closet 押入
30. living room 居間
31. bedroom 寝室

1. tree 木
2. leaf 葉
3. lawn / grass 芝生
4. lawn mower 芝刈り機
5. lounge chair レジャー椅子
6. wading pool 子供用プール
7. barbecue バーベキュー
8. patio 中庭
9. umbrella 日傘
10. (patio) table （中庭）テーブル
11. (patio) chair （中庭）椅子
12. bush 低木
13. flower bed 花壇

14. hedge 生垣
15. vegetable garden 野菜畑
16. watering can じょうろ
17. rake 熊手
18. trowel 移植ごて
19. rose バラ
20. daisy ひなぎく
21. azalea つつじ
22. snapdragon 金魚草
23. pansy パンジー
24. geranium ゼラニウム
25. tulip チューリップ
26. daffodil 水仙

1. couch / sofa ソファー
2. cushion クッション
3. (throw) pillow
   クッション
4. club chair ソファー
5. love seat
   二人掛けのソファー
6. coffee table
   コーヒーテーブル
7. end table
   エンドテーブル

8. lamp 電気スタンド
9. lamp shade
   ランプの傘
10. wall unit 戸棚ユニット
11. bookcase 本棚
12. book 本
13. window 窓
14. drape カーテン
15. plant 植物
16. planter プランター
17. flowers 花
18. vase 花びん
19. fireplace 暖炉
20. (fireplace) screen
    (暖炉) スクリーン

21. mantel マントル
22. picture 写真
23. (picture) frame 額
24. side table
    サイドテーブル
25. ottoman
    (背のない) 長椅子
26. rug 敷き物
27. floor 床
28. ceiling 天井

1. centerpiece センターピース
2. wine glass ワイングラス
3. water glass グラス
4. napkin ring ナプキンリング
5. napkin ナプキン
6. plate 皿
7. (dining room) table テーブル
8. chair 椅子
9. armchair ひじかけ椅子
10. (salad) fork (サラダ) フォーク
11. (dinner) fork (ディナー) フォーク
12. knife ナイフ
13. soupspoon スープスプーン
14. teaspoon ティースプーン
15. (serving) bowl 盛り鉢
16. server ワゴン
17. cup ティーカップ
18. saucer ソーサー
19. teapot ティーポット
20. sideboard / buffet サイドボード
21. mirror 鏡
22. chandelier シャンデリア

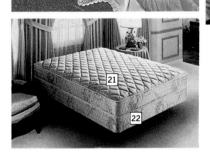

1. night table / nightstand
   ナイトテーブル
2. headboard
   ヘッドボード
3. throw pillow
   クッション
4. bed ベッド
5. bedspread
   ベッドカバー
6. dust ruffle
   ほこり除け
7. carpet
   カーペット
8. lamp 電気スタンド
9. chest (of drawers)
   たんす
10. drawer 引き出し
11. handle / pull
    とっ手

12. mirror 鏡
13. dresser ドレッサー
14. pillowcase 枕カバー
15. pillow 枕
16. (fitted) sheet
    フィットシーツ
17. (flat) sheet シーツ
18. comforter / quilt
    掛けぶとん
19. electric blanket
    電気毛布
20. (heat) control
    温度調節器
21. mattress マットレス
22. box spring
    スプリングマット

1. guest towel ゲストタオル
2. soap dispenser
   石鹸容器
3. hand towel タオル
4. tile タイル
5. bathtub / tub 浴槽
6. bath towel バスタオル
7. bath mat / bath rug
   バスマット
8. toilet トイレ
9. shelf 棚
10. light switch
    電灯スイッチ
11. towel rack タオルかけ
12. doorknob ドアノブ
13. toilet paper
    トイレットペーパー
14. mirror 鏡

15. medicine cabinet 薬品棚
16. cup コップ
17. toothbrush 歯ブラシ
18. toothbrush holder
    歯ブラシさし
19. soap 石鹸
20. soap dish 石鹸皿
21. sink 洗面台
22. hot water faucet 温水コック
23. cold water faucet 冷水コック
24. shower head シャワーヘッド
25. shower curtain rod
    シャワーカーテンレール
26. shower curtain シャワーカーテン
27. washcloth ボディタオル

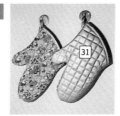

1. oven　オーブン
2. spice rack　スパイスラック
3. spices　香辛料
4. canister　小型つぼ
5. trivet　ごとく
6. sink　流し
7. faucet　蛇口
8. cake stand　ケーキスタンド
9. cookbook　料理の本
10. freezer　冷凍庫
11. refrigerator　冷蔵庫
12. dishwasher　皿洗い機
13. stove / range　レンジ
14. burner　コンロ
15. (copper) pot　鍋
16. coffee pot　コーヒーポット
17. creamer　クリーマー
18. cup　カップ
19. saucer　受皿
20. counter　カウンター
21. bowl　茶わん
22. plate　皿
23. drawer　引き出し
24. cupboard / cabinet
    戸棚／キャビネット
25. (door) handle　(ドア) とっ手
26. cutting board　まな板
27. (paring) knife　(果物) ナイフ
28. dish towel　ふきん
29. Saran wrap / plastic wrap
    サランラップ
30. aluminum foil　アルミホイル
31. pot holder　なべつかみ

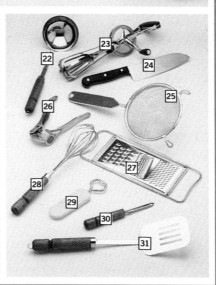

1. double boiler 二重なべ
2. lid / cover ふた
3. pot なべ
4. casserole キャセロール
5. frying pan / skillet
   フライパン
6. handle 柄
7. roaster ロースター
8. cake pan ケーキ型
9. bowl ボール
10. cookie sheet
    天板
11. rolling pin めん棒
12. measuring cup 計量カップ
13. measuring spoon 計量スプーン
14. coffee maker コーヒーメーカー
15. microwave oven 電子レンジ
16. can opener 缶切り
17. blender ジューサー
18. food processor
    フードプロセッサー
19. toaster oven
    オーブントースター
20. (electric) mixer
    電気かくはん器
21. toaster トースター
22. ladle しゃくし
23. (hand) beater / egg beater
    (手動) かくはん器 / (電動) 卵とき器
24. knife ナイフ
25. strainer 水切り
26. garlic press にんにくつぶし器
27. grater おろし金
28. whisk 泡立て器
29. bottle opener 栓ぬき
30. peeler 皮むき
31. spatula フライ返し

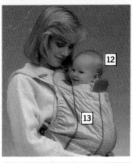

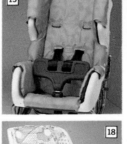
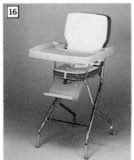

1. changing pad
   おむつ換えマット
2. child　子供
3. bar　柵
4. crib　ベビーベッド
5. chest (of drawers)　たんす
6. lamp　電気スタンド
7. teddy bear　熊のぬいぐるみ
8. stuffed animal
   動物のぬいぐるみ
9. baby chair　幼児用椅子
10. rug　じゅうたん
11. stroller　ベビーカー
12. baby / infant　赤ちゃん/幼児
13. baby carrier　ベビーキャリア
14. carriage　乳母車
15. car seat　幼児用カーシート
16. highchair　ベビーチェア
17. playpen　ベビーサークル
18. baby seat　ベビーシート
19. bib　よだれかけ
20. nipple　乳首
21. (baby) bottle　ほ乳びん
22. cap / top　ふた
23. food warmer　フードウォーマー
24. (baby) clothes　(ベビー) 服
25. diaper　おむつ

THE PLAYGROUND 児童公園

1. see-saw / teeter-totter シーソー
2. slide すべり台
3. toddler / child 幼児／子供
4. tricycle 三輪車
5. swing ぶらんこ
6. bench ベンチ
7. jungle gym ジャングルジム
8. sandbox 砂場
9. sand 砂
10. pail バケツ
11. shovel スコップ
12. overalls つなぎ服
13. sneakers 運動靴
14. water fountain 噴水
15. doll 人形
16. doll carriage おもちゃの乳母車
17. skateboard スケートボード
18. kite たこ

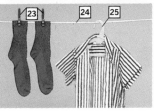

1. iron アイロン
2. ironing board
   アイロン台
3. scrub brush たわし
4. dust cloth ぞうきん
5. dustpan ちりとり
6. whisk broom 手ぼうき
7. broom ほうき
8. carpet sweeper
   カーペットクリーナー
9. vacuum cleaner
   掃除機
10. (sponge) mop
    (スポンジ) モップ

11. (dust) mop
    (ほこり取り) モップ
12. (wet) mop モップ
13. bucket/pail バケツ
14. sponge スポンジ
15. washer/washing
    machine 洗濯器
16. dryer 乾燥機
17. detergent 洗剤
18. measuring cup
    計量カップ
19. laundry 洗濯物
20. hamper 洗濯カゴ
21. laundry bag 洗濯バッグ

22. laundry basket
    洗濯バスケット
23. clothespin 洗濯ばさみ
24. clothesline 物干し綱
25. hanger ハンガー
26. three-pronged plug 三股プラグ
27. (wall) socket/outlet コンセント
28. (light) bulb 電球
29. extension cord
    延長コード

TOOLS 工具類

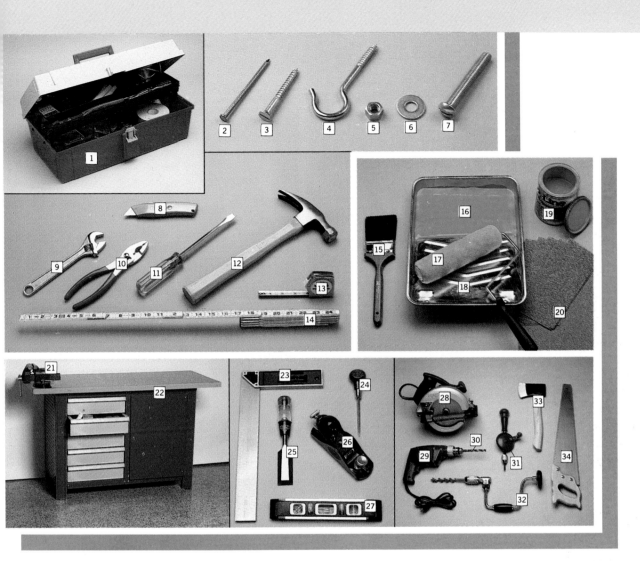

1. toolbox 工具箱
2. nail 釘
3. screw
   ねじ釘
4. hook フック
5. nut ナット
6. washer
   ワッシャー
7. bolt ボルト
8. utility knife
   万能ナイフ
9. wrench
   モンキースパナ

10. pliers ペンチ
11. screwdriver
    ドライバー
12. hammer 金づち
13. tape measure
    巻尺
14. folding rule
    折り尺
15. paintbrush/
    brush はけ
16. paint ペンキ
17. (paint) roller
    (ペンキ) ローラー

18. pan バット
19. (paint) can
    (ペンキ) カン
20. sandpaper
    サンドペーパー
21. vise 万力
22. workbench
    作業台
23. square 曲尺
24. awl 突きぎり
25. chisel のみ
26. plane かんな

27. level 水準器
28. power saw
    電気のこぎり
29. electric drill
    電気ドリル
30. bit 刃
31. hand drill
    ハンドドリル
32. brace
    曲りドリル
33. hatchet おの
34. saw のこぎり

1. video cassette recorder/VCR
   ビデオ/VCR
2. (video) cassette （ビデオ）カセット
3. remote control リモコン
4. television/TV テレビ/TV
5. screen 画面
6. stereo system ステレオシステム
7. record レコード
8. turntable 回転盤
9. amplifier アンプ
10. tuner チューナー
11. tape deck/cassette deck
    テープデッキ/カセットデッキ
12. speaker スピーカー
13. compact disc player
    コンパクトディスクプレーヤー

14. compact disc/CD
    コンパクトディスク/CD
15. radio ラジオ
16. clock radio 時計つきラジオ
17. tape recorder/cassette player
    テープレコーダー/カセットプレーヤー
18. personal cassette player/
    Walkman ウォークマン
19. headphone ヘッドホン
20. (audio) cassette/tape
    カセット/テープ
21. answering machine 留守番電話
22. telephone 電話

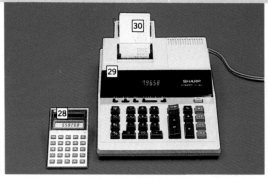

23. computer コンピューター
24. display screen / monitor
　　スクリーン / モニター
25. floppy disc / diskette
　　フロッピィーディスク／デイスケット
26. keyboard キーボード
27. printer プリンター
28. pocket calculator 小型計算機
29. calculator 計算機
30. tape ロールペーパー
31. adapter アダプター／整流器
32. battery 電池
33. voltage converter 変圧器
34. plug converter プラグコンバーター

35. electronic typewriter
　　電子タイプライター
36. electric typewriter
　　電動タイプライター
37. disc camera ディスクカメラ
38. disc film ディスクフィルム
39. camera カメラ
40. lens レンズ
41. flash フラッシュ
42. film フィルム
43. video camera ビデオカメラ
44. slide projector
　　スライドプロジェクター

CONSTRUCTION　建設

1. construction worker
   建設工事作業員
2. hook　フック
3. girder　梁
4. ladder　はしご
5. hard hat　ヘルメット
6. tool belt　工具ベルト
7. scaffold　足場
8. crane　クレーン
9. excavation site　掘削現場
10. dump truck
    ダンプカー
11. frontend loader
    前面積み込み機
12. backhoe　ショベルカー
13. blasting mat
    爆破マット
14. cement mixer
    コンクリートミキサー／ミキサー車
15. cement　セメント
16. trowel　こて
17. brick　れんが
18. level　水準器
19. wheelbarrow　手押し車
20. jack hammer／
    pneumatic drill
    削岩機
21. shovel　シャベル
22. sledge hammer
    ハンマー
23. pick ax　つるはし

LAND & WATER 大地と水

1. mountain 山
2. peak 山頂
3. meadow 草原
4. valley 渓谷
5. hill 丘
6. tree 木
7. grass 草地
8. field 野原
9. cliff がけ
10. rock 岩
11. forest 森
12. lake 湖
13. pond 池
14. river 川
15. stream／brook 谷川
16. waterfall 滝
17. desert 砂漠
18. dune 砂丘

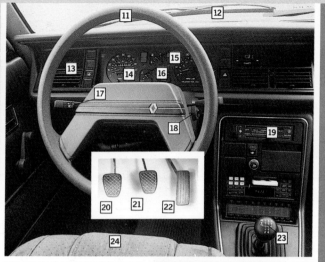

1. gas station
   ガソリンスタンド
2. gas pump　燃料ポンプ
3. nozzle　ノズル
4. hose　ホース
5. attendant　係員
6. (rear) windshield
   (後) ガラス
7. trunk　トランク
8. license plate
   ナンバープレート
9. taillight　尾灯
10. bumper　バンパー
11. steering wheel
   ハンドル
12. windshield wiper
   ワイパー
13. dashboard/
   instrument panel
   ダッシュボード/計器盤

14. speedometer　速度計
15. fuel gauge　燃料計
16. temperature gauge
   温度ゲージ
17. turn signal
   方向指示器
18. ignition　イグニション
19. heater　ヒーター
20. clutch　クラッチ
21. brake　ブレーキ
22. gas pedal/
   accelerator　アクセル
23. gearshift　ギア
24. seat　シート
25. heater hose
   ヒーターホース
26. air filter
   エアフィルター
27. battery　バッテリー
28. engine　エンジン

29. alternator
   交流発電機
30. cool air duct
   冷風ダクト
31. coolant recovery
   tank　冷却液タンク
32. radiator　ラジエーター
33. sedan　セダン
34. hubcap
   ホイールキャップ
35. tire　タイヤ
36. convertible
   コンバーチブル
37. station wagon
   ステーションワゴン
38. pick-up truck
   小型トラック

A. The Train Station 駅

1. information booth
   案内係詰め所
2. clock 時計
3. ticket counter
   切符売場
4. arrival and departure board
   出発到着案内板
5. train 列車
6. track 線路

7. platform
   プラットフォーム
8. passenger car 客車
9. porter / redcap
   ポーター
10. passenger 乗客

B. The Bus Station バスターミナル

11. bus バス
12. driver 運転士
13. suitcase スーツケース
14. luggage compartment
    荷物入れ

C. The Taxi Stand タクシー乗場

15. taxi タクシー
16. radio call sign
    無線呼出標示
17. off-duty sign
    勤務外標示
18. (door) handle
    (ドア) 取っ手
19. door ドア

D. Schedule 時刻表

PELHAM TO NEW YORK

MONDAY TO FRIDAY, EXCEPT HOLIDAYS					
Leave	Arrive	Leave	Arrive	Leave	Arrive
Pelham	New York	Pelham	New York	Pelham	New York
AM	AM	AM	AM	PM	PM
5:32	6:00	F10:40	F11:10	FY 5:33	F 6:03
6:02	6:30	11:03	11:33	6:03	6:33
6:32	7:00	11:33	12:03	F 6:33	F 7:03
6:52	7:20	12:03	12:33	7:03	7:33
7:12	7:40	F12:33	F 1:03	F 7:33	F 8:03
7:28	X 8:00	1:03	1:33	Y 8:03	8:33
F 7:44	F 8:14	1:33	2:03	F 8:33	F 9:03
7:59	8:28	2:03	2:33	9:03	9:33
8:17	8:46	F 2:33	F 3:03	9:35	10:03
F 8:32	F 9:01	3:03	3:33	F10:33	F11:03
F 9:05	F 9:35	F 3:33	F 4:03	11:33	12:03
F 9:22	F 9:52	4:03	4:33	12:58	1:28
9:43	10:12	F 4:33	F 5:03	....	....
F10:03	F10:33	Y 5:03	5:33		
AM	AM	PM	PM	PM	AM

SATURDAY, SUNDAY & HOLIDAYS					
AM	AM	PM	PM	PM	PM
7:03	7:33	12:33	1:03	6:33	7:03
8:03	8:33	F 1:33	F 2:03	F 7:33	F 8:03
8:33	F 9:03	2:33	3:03	8:33	9:03
S 9:03	S 9:33	F 3:33	F 4:03	F 9:33	F10:03
9:33	F10:03	4:33	5:03	10:33	11:03
F10:03	F10:33	S 5:03	S 5:33	11:33	12:03
F11:33	F12:03	F 5:33	F 6:03	12:58	1:28
AM	PM	PM	PM	AM	AM

A. Highway 高速道路
1. overpass 高架道路橋
2. underpass 車両用地下道
3. broken line （車線境界線）破線
4. solid line 実線
5. shoulder 路肩
6. divider 中央分離帯
7. left lane 左側車線
8. middle lane 中央車線
9. right lane 右側車線
10. van 小型トラック
11. car 車
12. bus バス
13. truck トラック

B. Tollgate 料金所
14. tollbooth 料金徴収所
15. exact change lane
    釣銭不要のレーン
16. change lane 釣銭用レーン

C. Tunnel トンネル
17. street light 街灯

D. Bridge 橋

E. Road 道路
18. dirt road 舗装されていない道路
19. curve sign カーブ標識
20. double yellow lines
    追い越禁止線

F. Intersection 交差点
21. crosswalk 横断歩道
22. street 道路
23. corner コーナー

G. Railroad Crossing 踏切
24. traffic light 信号
25. railroad track 鉄道車線

H. Road Signs 道路標識
26. route sign 道路番号標識
27. stop sign 一時停止標識
28. yield sign 前方優先道路標識
29. do not enter sign 進入禁止標識
30. school crossing sign
    学童横断標識
31. speed limit sign 速度制限標識
32. no U-turn sign Uターン禁止標識
33. no left turn sign 左折禁止標識
34. no right turn sign 右折禁止標識
35. no trucks sign
    トラック通行禁止標識
36. hill sign 下り坂標識
37. slippery when wet sign
    雨天時スリップ注意
38. telephone sign 公衆電話標識
39. bike route sign 自転車専用路標識

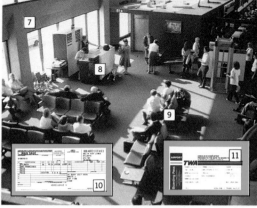

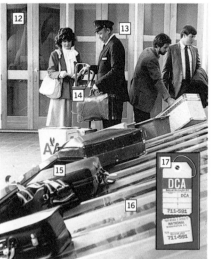

A. The Terminal
ターミナル

1. ticket agent 航空券係
2. ticket counter
 チケットカウンター
3. suitcase スーツケース
4. arrival and departure
 board 出発到着案内板
5. security check
 手荷物検査
6. security guard
 手荷物検査係
7. gate ゲート
8. check-in counter
 チェックインカウンター
9. waiting room 待合室
10. ticket 航空券
11. boarding pass 搭乗券
12. baggage claim area
 手荷物受取所
13. porter / skycap
 ポーター
14. luggage carrier
 キャリアー
15. luggage 旅行手荷物
16. (luggage) carousel
 (荷物) 回転式コンベヤー
17. (baggage) claim
 check 手荷物受取札
18. customs 税関
19. customs officer
 税関職員
20. documents 書類
21. passport 旅券

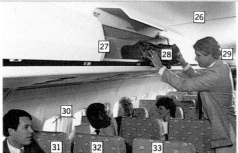

B. On Board
機内

22. cockpit 操縦室
23. pilot/captain
    パイロット/機長
24. co-pilot 副操縦士
25. instrument panel
    計器盤
26. cabin 客室
27. overhead (luggage)
    compartment 頭上
    (荷物) コンパートメント
28. carry-on   luggage/
    carry-on bag
    手荷物/手さげかばん
29. passenger 乗客
30. window 窓
31. window seat 窓側座席
32. middle seat 中央座席
33. aisle seat 通路側座席
34. flight attendant 搭乗員
35. tray table テーブル
36. tray トレー
37. armrest ひじかけ

C. The Runway
滑走路

38. terminal ターミナル
39. jet (plane) 飛行機
40. tail 尾翼
41. jet engine
    ジェットエンジン
42. wing 主翼
43. runway 滑走路
44. control tower 管制塔
45. rotor ローター/回転翼
46. helicopter
    ヘリコプター
47. hangar 格納庫

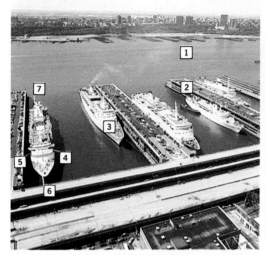

1. harbor 港
2. pier/dock 桟橋/波止場
3. passenger ship/
   ocean liner 客船
4. port 左舷
5. starboard 右舷
6. bow 船首
7. stern 船尾
8. cargo ship/freighter 貨物船
9. cargo 積荷/貨物
10. deck デッキ
11. winch 巻揚機
12. line 綱
13. derrick 積荷用起重機
14. dock worker/
    longshoreman 港湾労働者
15. crane クレーン
16. (oil) tanker (原油)タンカー
17. buoy ブイ
18. barge はしけ
19. tugboat タグボート
20. ferry フェリー

THE BEACH 海辺

1. hotel ホテル
2. boardwalk 遊歩道
3. sand 砂
4. (beach) blanket ビーチマット
5. (beach) towel ビーチタオル
6. trash can ゴミ入れ
7. (beach) chair ビーチチェア
8. (beach) umbrella
   ビーチパラソル
9. lounge chair テッキチェア
10. lifeguard stand
    水難監視スタンド

11. lifeguard 水難監視員
12. wave 波
13. ocean 海
14. (beach) ball ビーチボール
15. (beach) hat/sun hat
    ビーチハット
16. sand castle 砂の城
17. bathing suit 水着
18. pail/bucket バケツ
19. seashell 貝
20. rock 石

WATER SPORTS　ウォータースポーツ

A. Swimming
水泳
1. swimmer　泳いでいる人
2. swimming pool　プール

B. Diving
ダイビング/飛び込み
3. diver　ダイバー/
　　飛び込み選手
4. diving board　飛び込み板

C. Snorkeling
シュノーケル
5. snokeler
　　シュノーケルをする人
6. snorkel　シュノーケル

D. Scuba Diving
スキューバダイビング
7. scuba diver
　　スキューバダイバー

8. wet suit　ウェットスーツ
9. (air) tank　空気ボンベ
10. mask　マスク

E. Fishing　釣り
11. fisherman　釣師
12. fishing rod　釣ざお
13. (fishing) line　釣糸

F. Surfing
サーフィン
14. surfer　サーファー
15. surf　波
16. surfboard　サーフボード

G. Windsurfing
ウィンドサーフィン
17. windsurfer　ウィンド
　　サーフィンをする人
18. sail　帆

H. Sailing
セーリング
19. sailboat　ヨット
20. mast　マスト

I. Waterskiing
水上スキー
21. water-skier
　　水上スキーヤー
22. water ski　水上スキー
23. towrope　引き綱
24. motorboat
　　モーターボート

J. Rowing
ボートこぎ
25. rower　こぎ手
26. rowboat　こぎ船
27. oar　オール

K. Canoeing
カヌー
28. canoeist　カヌーのこぎ手
29. canoe　カヌー
30. paddle　かい

L. Kayaking
カヤック
31. kayaker
　　カヤックをする人
32. kayak　カヤック

M. White Water Rafting
急流川下り
33. raft　ゴムボート
34. life jacket
　　救命胴衣
35. rapids　急流

WINTER SPORTS 冬のスポーツ

A. Sledding そり
1. sled そり

B. Downhill Skiing 滑降スキー
2. skier スキーヤー
3. pole ストック
4. (ski) boot スキーブーツ
5. ski スキー
6. chair lift リフト

C. Cross Country Skiing クロスカントリースキー
7. skier スキーヤー
8. ski cap スキー帽
9. trail 道

D. Figure Skating フィギュアスケート
10. figure skater フィギュアスケーター
11. figure skate フィギュアスケート
12. blade ブレード

E. Ice Skating アイスケート
13. skater スケートをする人
14. skate スケート
15. ice 氷

F. Bobsledding ボブスレー
16. bobsled ボブスレー
17. helmet ヘルメット

G. Snowmobiling スノーモービル
18. snowmobile スノーモービル

SPECTATOR SPORTS 観戦スポーツ

12. third baseman 三塁手
13. coach コーチ
14. third base 三塁
15. home (plate) 本塁
16. umpire アンパイヤー
17. spectator 観客
18. baseball 野球ボール
19. batter バッター
20. bat バット
21. helmet ヘルメット
22. uniform ユニフォーム
23. catcher 捕手
24. mask マスク
25. (baseball) glove/
    mitt グローブ/ミット
26. shin guard すね当て

B. Football
フットボール

27. (football) field
    (フットボール) 競技場
28. fullback/runningback
    フルバック
29. halfback/runningback
    ハーフバック
30. right end/wide
    receiver ライトエンド
31. tight end タイトエンド
32. right tackle
    ライトタックル
33. right guard
    ライトガード
34. center センター
35. quarterback
    クオーターバック
36. left guard レフトガード
37. left tackle
    レフトタックル
38. left end/wide
    receiver レフトエンド
39. football フットボール

A. Baseball
野球

1. stadium 野球場
2. stadium lights 照明
3. foul line ファウルライン
4. (pitcher's) mound
   (ピッチャー) マウンド
5. pitcher ピッチャー
6. first base 一塁
7. first baseman 一塁手
8. outfielder 外野手
9. second baseman
   二塁手
10. second base 二塁
11. shortstop ショート

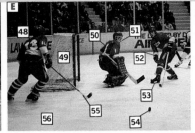

49. goal ゴール
50. goalie ゴールキーパー
51. mask マスク
52. glove グローブ
53. skate スケート
54. puck パック
55. (hockey) stick
(ホッケー) スティック
56. ice 氷

F. Tennis テニス
57. (tennis) player
テニスの選手
58. (tennis) racket (テニス)
ラケット
59. (tennis) ball
(テニス) ボール
60. net ネット
61. (tennis) court
(テニス) コート
62. baseline ベースライン

G. Wrestling レスリング
63. wrestler レスリング選手
64. mat マット

H. Karate 空手
65. (black) belt (黒) 帯

I. Boxing ボクシング
66. boxer
ボクサー/ボクシングの選手
67. (boxing) glove
(ボクシング) グローブ
68. trunks トランクス
69. referee レフリー
70. rope ロープ
71. ring リング

J. Horse Racing 競馬
72. gate ゲート

C. Basketball バスケットボール
40. (basketball) player
バスケット選手
41. basketball
バスケットボール
42. backboard
バックボード
43. basket バスケット

D. Soccer サッカー
44. (soccer) player
(サッカー) 選手
45. goal ゴール
46. (soccer) ball
(サッカー) ボール
47. (soccer) field
(サッカー) 競技場

E. Ice Hockey アイスホッケー
48. (hockey) player
(ホッケー) 選手

OTHER SPORTS　その他のスポーツ

A. Jogging
ジョギング

1. jogger　ジョガー

B. Running
ランニング

2. runner　ランナー

C. Cycling
サイクリング

3. cyclist　サイクリスト
4. helmet　ヘルメット
5. bicycle/bike　自転車
6. (bicycle) pack
   自転車用かご
7. wheel　車輪

D. Horseback Riding　乗馬

8. (horseback) rider
   (馬の) 乗り手
9. horse　馬
10. reins　手綱
11. saddle　サドル
12. stirrup　あぶみ

E. Archery
アーチェリー

13. archer　射手
14. bow　弓
15. arrow　矢
16. target　標的

F. Golf　ゴルフ

17. golfer　ゴルファー
18. (golf) club
    (ゴルフ) クラブ
19. (golf) ball　(ゴルフ) ボール
20. hole　ホール
21. green　グリーン

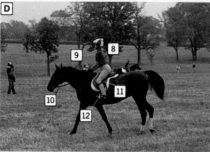

G. Hiking
ハイキング

22. hiker　ハイカー
23. backpack　バックパック
24. hiking boot
    ハイキングシューズ
25. trail　道

H. Camping
キャンピング

26. camper　キャンパー
27. tent　テント

I. Volleyball バレーボール

28. (volleyball) player
(バレーボール) 選手
29. volleyball バレーボール
30. net ネット

J. Rollerskating
ローラースケート

31. roller skater ローラースケーター
32. roller skate ローラースケート
33. rink リンク

K. Bowling ボウリング

34. bowler ボウラー
35. (bowling) ball (ボウリング) ボール
36. gutter ガター
37. alley レーン
38. pin ピン

L. Ping Pong / Table
Tennis 卓球

39. (ping pong) player (卓球) 選手
40. paddle ラケット
41. (ping pong) ball (卓球) ボール
42. net ネット
43. (ping pong) table (卓球) テーブル

M. Handball ハンドボール

44. (handball) player (ハンドボール) 選手
45. glove グローブ

N. Squash スカッシュ

46. (squash) player
(スカッシュ) の選手
47. (squash) racket
(スカッシュ) ラケット
48. (squash) ball (スカッシュ) ボール

O. Racquetball
ラケットボール

49. (racquetball) player
(ラケットボール) の選手
50. (racquetball) racket
(ラケットボール) ラケット
51. racquetball ラケットボール
52. court コート

ENTERTAINMENT エンターテインメント

A. Symphony 交響楽
1. orchestra オーケストラ
2. podium 指揮台
3. conductor 指揮者
4. (sheet) music 楽譜
5. music stand 譜面台

B. Opera オペラ
6. chorus コーラス
7. singer 歌手

C. Ballet バレエ
8. ballerina バレリーナ
9. ballet dancer バレエダンサー
10. toe shoe トーシューズ

D. Theater 劇場
11. actress 女優
12. actor 男優
13. stage 舞台
14. audience 観客
15. aisle 通路
16. spotlight スポットライト
17. footlights フットライト
18. orchestra pit 楽団席

E. Movie Theater 映画館
19. marqee 入り口のひさし
20. billboard 広告掲示板

F. Rock Concert ロックコンサート
21. singer / vocalist シンガー／ボーカリスト

MUSICAL INSTRUMENTS 楽器

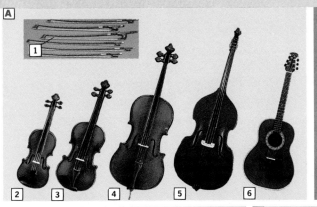

A. Strings 弦楽器
1. bow 弓
2. violin バイオリン
3. viola ビオラ
4. cello チェロ
5. bass コントラバス/ベース
6. guitar ギター

B. Brass 金管楽器
7. trombone トロンボーン
8. French horn フレンチホルン
9. tuba チューバ
10. trumpet トランペット

C. Woodwinds 木管楽器
11. flute フルート
12. recorder リコーダー
13. oboe オーボエ
14. clarinet クラリネット
15. saxophone サキソホーン
16. bassoon バスーン

D. Percussion 打楽器
17. cymbal シンバル
18. drum ドラム
19. xylophone 木琴

E. Other Instruments その他の楽器
20. piano ピアノ
21. accordion アコーディオン
22. harmonica ハーモニカ

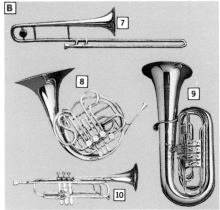
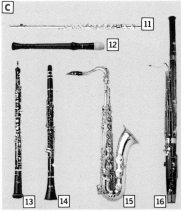
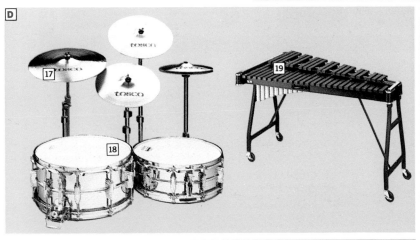
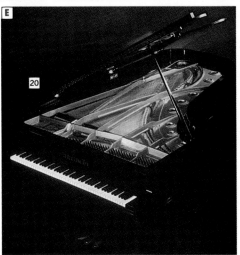

THE ZOO & PETS 動物園、ペット

A. The Zoo
動物園
1. lion ライオン
2. mane たてがみ
3. tiger トラ
4. paw 足
5. tail 尾
6. leopard ヒョウ
7. spot 斑点
8. elephant 象
9. tusk きば
10. trunk 鼻
11. rhinoceros サイ
12. horn つの
13. hippopotamus カバ
14. bear クマ
15. polar bear 白熊
16. buffalo
    野牛/バッファロー
17. zebra しま馬
18. stripe しま
19. camel ラクダ
20. hump こぶ
21. giraffe キリン
22. deer シカ
23. antler 枝角
24. llama ラマ
25. koala bear コアラ
26. kangaroo カンガルー
27. pouch 腹袋
28. monkey サル
29. gorilla ゴリラ
30. fox キツネ
31. raccoon アライグマ

32. alligator ワニ
33. snake ヘビ
34. tortoise (陸棲) カメ
35. lizard トカゲ
36. frog カエル
37. turtle (ウミ) カメ

B. Pets ペット

38. puppy 子犬
39. dog 犬
40. paw 足
41. kitten 子猫
42. cat 猫

43. whiskers ひげ
44. parrot オウム
45. parakeet インコ
46. gerbil アレチネズミ
47. tail 尾
48. hamster ハムスター
49. guinea pig
    テンジクネズミ／モルモット
50. rabbit うさぎ
51. goldfish 金魚
52. (fish) bowl (金魚) 鉢
53. tropical fish 熱帯魚

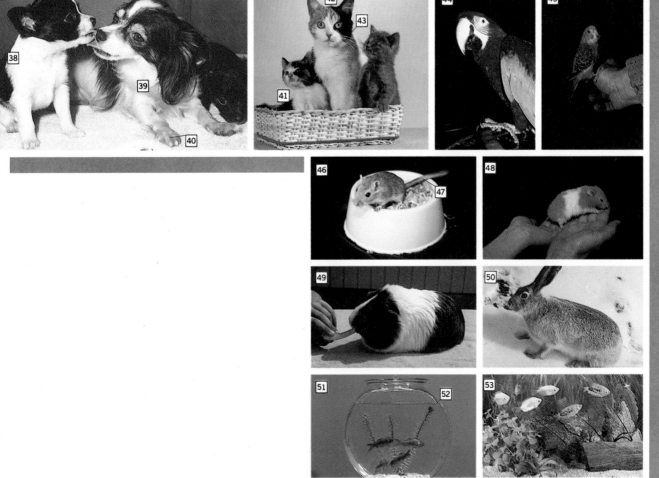

THE FARM 農場

1. farmland 農地
2. farmhouse 農家
3. barn 納屋
4. silo サイロ
5. barnyard 納屋の前庭
6. fence 柵
7. pond 池
8. wheat field 小麦畑
9. combine コンバイン
10. vegetable field 野菜畑
11. farmer 農夫
12. tractor トラクター
13. furrow あぜ溝

14. crop 作物
15. irrigation system 灌漑装置
16. horse 馬
17. mane たてがみ
18. pig 豚
19. piglet 子豚
20. pigpen / pig sty 養豚場
21. cow 雌牛
22. calf 子牛
23. bull 雄牛

24. sheep 羊
25. lamb 小羊
26. goat ヤギ
27. kid 子ヤギ
28. chicken / hen 鶏/めんどり
29. chick ヒヨコ
30. rooster 雄鶏

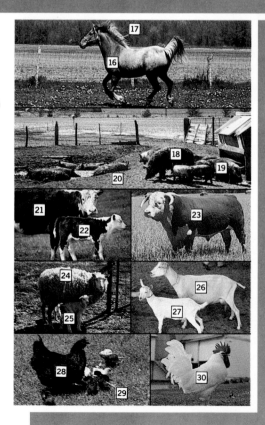

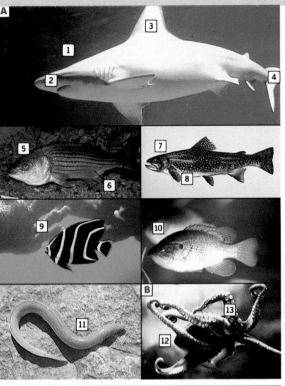

A. Fish 魚

1. shark サメ
2. snout 鼻
3. fin ひれ
4. tail 尾
5. bass スズキ
6. scale 鱗
7. trout マス
8. gill 鰓
9. angelfish エンゼルフィッシュ
10. sunfish サンフィッシュ
11. eel ウナギ

B. Sea Animals 海洋動物

12. octopus タコ
13. tentacle 触腕
14. whale 鯨
15. dolphin イルカ
16. seal アザラシ
17. flipper ひれ足
18. walrus セイウチ
19. tusk 牙
20. turtle （ウミ）カメ
21. lobster ロブスター
22. shrimp 子エビ
23. mussel ムール貝
24. crab カニ
25. claw はさみ
26. clam 二枚貝
27. starfish ヒトデ

1. flamingo フラミンゴ
2. pelican ペリカン
3. bill 喙
4. swan 白鳥
5. stork コウノトリ
6. crane ツル
7. gull カモメ
8. duck カモ
9. duckling カモの子
10. penguin ペンギン
11. flipper ペンギンの翼
12. crow カラス
13. ostrich ダチョウ
14. eagle ワシ
15. beak くちばし
16. hawk 鷹

17. claw かぎつめ
18. owl フクロウ
19. peacock クジャク
20. feather 羽根
21. pigeon ハト
22. pheasant キジ
23. tail 尾
24. robin コマツグミ
25. blue jay 青カケス
26. hummingbird ハチドリ
27. wing 翼
28. swallow ツバメ
29. cockatoo バタンインコ
30. crest カンムリ
31. nest 巣
32. egg 卵

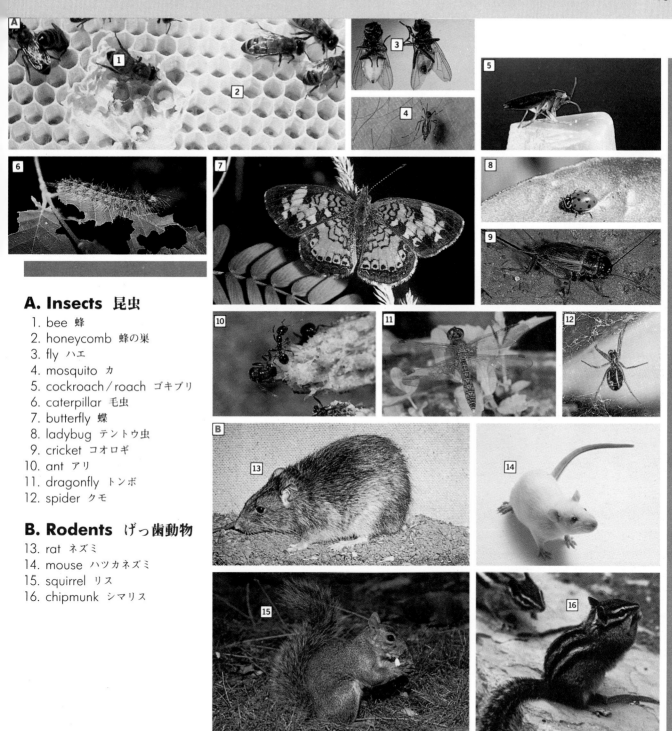

A. Insects 昆虫

1. bee 蜂
2. honeycomb 蜂の巣
3. fly ハエ
4. mosquito カ
5. cockroach / roach ゴキブリ
6. caterpillar 毛虫
7. butterfly 蝶
8. ladybug テントウ虫
9. cricket コオロギ
10. ant アリ
11. dragonfly トンボ
12. spider クモ

B. Rodents げっ歯動物

13. rat ネズミ
14. mouse ハツカネズミ
15. squirrel リス
16. chipmunk シマリス

SPACE 宇宙

1. galaxy　銀河
2. star　星
3. comet　彗星
4. Sun　太陽
5. planet / Saturn
　　惑星／土星
6. Earth　地球
7. Moon　月
8. astronaut　宇宙飛行士
9. space suit　宇宙服
10. flag　旗
11. lunar module　月着陸船
12. lunar vehicle　月面車
13. satellite　衛星、人工衛星
14. space shuttle
　　スペースシャトル
15. fuel tank　燃料タンク
16. booster rocket
　　ブースターロケット

THE MILITARY　軍　隊

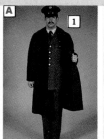

A. Army　陸軍

1. soldier　兵士
2. fatigues　戦闘服
3. camouflage　擬装
4. bayonet　銃剣
5. rifle　ライフル
6. machine gun　機関銃
7. jeep　ジープ
8. cannon　大砲
9. tank　戦車

B. Air Force　空軍

10. pilot　パイロット
11. parachute　パラシュート
12. parachutist　落下傘兵
13. helicopter　ヘリコプター
14. fighter plane　戦闘機
15. bomber　爆撃機
16. bomb　爆弾

C. Navy　海軍

17. sailor　水兵
18. submarine　潜水艦
19. destroyer　駆逐艦
20. radar antenna　レーダーアンテナ
21. battleship　戦艦
22. aircraft carrier　航空母艦

D. Marines　海兵隊

HOBBIES & GAMES 趣味とゲーム

A. Hobbies 趣味

1. coin collecting コイン収集
2. coin コイン
3. (coin) album (コイン) アルバム
4. coin catalog コインカタログ
5. magnifying glass 虫メガネ
6. stamp collecting 切手収集
7. (stamp) album (切手) アルバム
8. stamp 切手
9. stamp catalog 切手カタログ
10. photography 写真
11. camera カメラ
12. astronomy 天文学
13. telescope 望遠鏡
14. bird watching 野鳥観察

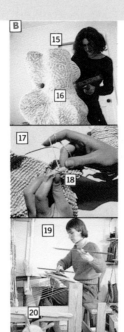

B. Crafts 工芸

15. sculpting 彫刻
16. sculpture 彫刻物
17. knitting 編物
18. knitting needle 編針
19. weaving 織物
20. loom はた (織)
21. pottery 陶芸
22. potter's wheel ろくろ
23. painting 絵画
24. brush 絵筆
25. woodworking 木工

C. Games ゲーム

26. chess チェス
27. board 盤
28. checkers チェッカー
29. backgammon バックギャモン
30. Scrabble スクラブル
31. Monopoly モノポリー
32. cards トランプ

SEWING & SUNDRIES　裁縫と雑貨品

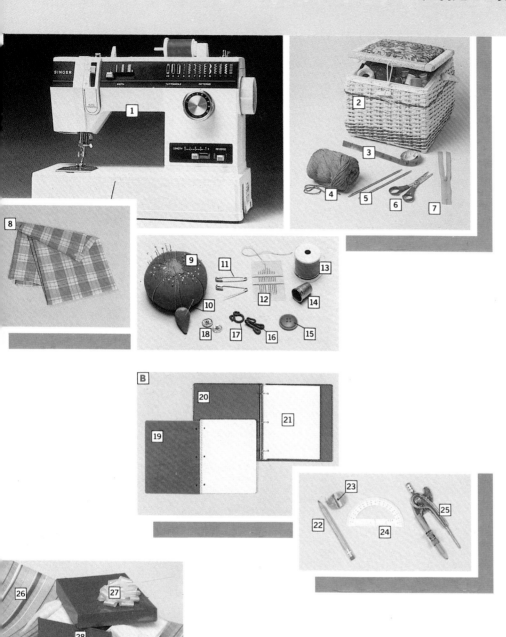

A. Sewing　裁縫

1. sewing machine　ミシン
2. sewing basket　裁縫箱
3. tape measure　テープメジャー
4. yarn　毛糸
5. knitting needle　編針
6. (pair of) scissors　鋏
7. zipper　ファスナー
8. material　布地
9. pin cushion　針山
10. straight pin　まち針
11. safety pin　安全ピン
12. needle　縫針
13. thread　糸
14. thimble　指ぬき
15. button　ボタン
16. hook　ホック
17. eye　ホック受け
18. snap　ホック

B. Sundries　雑貨品

19. (spiral) notebook　（らせんとじ）ノート
20. loose-leaf binder　ルーズリーフバインダー
21. (loose-leaf) paper　ルーズリーフ紙
22. pencil　鉛筆
23. pencil sharpener　鉛筆削り
24. protractor　分度器
25. compass　コンパス
26. wrapping paper　包み紙
27. bow　ちょう結び
28. box　箱
29. tissue paper　ティッシュペーパー
30. ribbon　リボン
31. string　ひも
32. masking tape　マスキングテープ

video camera
/ˈvɪdiˠoʷ ˌkæmərə/ **52-43**
video cassette
/ˈvɪdiˠoʷ kəˈsɛt/ **51-2**
video cassette recorder
/ˈvɪdiˠoʷ kəˈsɛt rɪˌkɔrdər/ **51-1**
Vietnam /ˌviˠɛtˈnɑm/ **8**
viola /viˠiˈoʷlə/ **70-3**
violin /ˌvaɪəˈlɪn/ **70-2**
Virginia /vərˈdʒɪnyə/ **9**
vise /vaɪs/ **50-21**
V-neck /ˈviˠ nɛk/ **37-11**
vocalist /ˈvoʷkəlɪst/ **69-21**
volleyball /ˈvaliˠˌbɔl/ **68-1, 29**
volleyball player
/ˈvaliˠbɔl ˌpleˠər/ **68-28**
voltage converter
/ˈvoʷltɪdʒ kənˌvɜrtər/ **52-33**

wading pool /ˈweˠdɪŋ ˌpuʷl/ **40-6**
waist /weˠst/ **23-30**
waiter /ˈweˠtər/ **21-22**
waiting room /ˈweˠtɪŋ ˌruʷm/
59-9
waitress /ˈweˠtrəs/ **21-23**
wake up /ˌweˠk ˈʌp/ **26-1**
walk /wɔk/ **27-6**
Walkman /ˈwɔkmən/ **51-18**
walk sign /ˈwɔk ˌsaɪn/ **11-16**
wallet /ˈwɑlət/ **38-29**
wall socket /ˈwɔl ˌsɑkɪt/ **49-27**
wall unit /ˈwɔl ˌyuʷnɪt/ **41-10**
walrus /ˈwɔlrəs/ **74-18**
warm /wɔrm/ **4-b**
wash your face
/ˌwɑʃ yər ˈfeˠs/ **26-8**
washcloth /ˈwɑʃklɔθ/ **44-27**
washer /ˈwɑʃər/ **49-15; 50-6**
washing machine
/ˈwɑʃɪŋ məˌʃiˠn/ **49-15**
Washington /ˈwɑʃɪŋtən/ **9**
wastepaper basket
/ˈweˠst ˌpeˠpər ˌbæskɪt/ **20-15**
watch /wɑtʃ/ **2-e, f; 26-17; 38-2**
watch TV /ˌwɑtʃ ˌtiˠ ˈviˠ/ **26-17**
water /ˈwɔtər/ **54**
watercress /ˈwɔtərˌkrɛs/ **16-4**
waterfall /ˈwɔtərˌfɔl/ **54-16**
water fountain /ˈwɔtər ˌfaʊntn/
48-14
waterfront /ˈwɔtərˌtrʌnt/ **61**
water glass /ˈwɔtər ˌglæs/ **42-3**
watering can /ˈwɔtərɪŋ ˌkæn/
40-16
watermelons /ˈwɔtərˌmɛlənz/
15-23
Water Pik /ˈwɔtər ˌpɪk/ **30-15**
water ski /ˈwɔtər ˌskiˠ/ **63-22**
water-skier /ˈwɔtər ˌskiˠər/ **63-21**
waterskiing /ˈwɔtərˌskiˠɪŋ/ **63-1**
water sports /ˈwɔtər ˌspɔrts/ **63**
wave /weˠv/ **28-20; 62-12**
weather /ˈwɛðər/ **4-B**
weaving /ˈwiˠvɪŋ/ **79-19**
Wednesday /ˈwɛnzdiˠ/ **3**
week /wiˠk/ **3-C**
welder /ˈwɛldər/ **21-9**
west /wɛst/ **9**
West Coast /ˌwɛst ˈkoʷst/ **9**
Western Canada
/ˌwɛstərn ˈkænədə/ **10**
Western Sahara
/ˌwɛstərn səˈhærə/ **8**
West Germany
/ˌwɛst ˈdʒɜrməniˠ/ **8**

West Virginia
/ˌwɛst vərˈdʒɪnyə/ **9**
wet /wɛt/ **33-21**
wet mop /ˈwɛt ˌmɑp/ **49-12**
wet suit /ˈwɛt suʷt/ **63-8**
whale /weˠl/ **74-14**
wheat field /ˈhwiˠt ˌfiˠld/ **73-8**
wheel /hwiˠl/ **67-7**
wheelbarrow /ˈhwiˠlˌbæroʷ/
53-19
whisk /hwɪsk/ **46-28**
whisk broom /ˈhwɪsk ˌbruʷm/
49-6
whiskers /ˈhwɪskərz/ **72-43**
white /hwaɪt/ **35-24**
white water rafting
/ˌhwaɪt ˌwɔtər ˈræftɪŋ/ **63-M**
wide /waɪd/ **34-39**
wide receiver /ˌwaɪd rɪˈsiˠvər/
65-30, 38
width /wɪdθ/ **5-14**
wife /waɪf/ **31**
winch /wɪntʃ/ **61-11**
window /ˈwɪndoʷ/ **39-8; 41-13;
60-30**
window seat /ˈwɪndoʷ ˌsiˠt/
60-31
window washer
/ˈwɪndoʷ ˌwɑʃər/ **21-5**
windshield /ˈwɪndʃiˠld/ **55-6**
windshield wiper
/ˈwɪndʃiˠld ˌwaɪpər/ **55-12**
windsurfer /ˈwɪndˌsɜrfər/ **63-17**
windsurfing /ˈwɪndˌsɜrfɪŋ/ **63-G**
windy /ˈwɪndiˠ/ **4-13**
wine glass /ˈwaɪn ˌglæs/ **42-2**
wing /wɪŋ/ **60-42; 75-27**
winter /ˈwɪntər/ **4-3**
winter sports /ˌwɪntər ˈspɔrts/
64
Wisconsin /wɪˈskɑnsɪn/ **9**
withdrawal slip
/wɪðˈdrɔəl ˌslɪp/ **6-12**
women's wear
/ˈwɪmɪnz ˌwɛər/ **36; 37**
woodwinds /ˈwʊdˌwɪndz/ **70-C**
woodworking /ˈwʊdˌwɜrkɪŋ/
79-25
workbench /ˈwɜrkbɛntʃ/ **50-22**
world /wɜrld/ **7**
worried /ˈwɔriˠd/ **32-17**
wrapping paper
/ˈræpɪŋ ˌpeˠpər/ **80-26**
wrench /rɛntʃ/ **50-9**
wrestler /ˈrɛslər/ **66-63**
wrestling /ˈrɛslɪŋ/ **66-G**
wrist /rɪst/ **23-13**
write /raɪt/ **28-1**
Wyoming /waɪˈoʷmɪŋ/ **9**

Xerox machine
/ˈzɪərɑks məˌʃiˠn/ **20-31**
x-ray /ˈɛks reˠ/ **29-5**
x-ray machine
/ˈɛks reˠ məˌʃiˠn/ **30-5**
xylophone /ˈzaɪləˌfoʷn/ **70-19**

yard /yɑrd/ **5-25**
yard stick /ˈyɑrdˌstɪk/ **5-24**
yarn /yɑrn/ **80-4**
year /yɪər/ **3-A**
yellow /ˈyɛloʷ/ **36-23**
yellow peppers
/ˌyɛloʷ ˈpɛpərz/ **16-8**

Yemen (Aden)
/ˈyɛmən/ (/ˈeˠdn/) **8**
Yemen (Sana) /ˈyɛmən/
(/ˈsɑnə/) **8**
yield sign /ˈyiəld ˌsaɪn/ **58-28**
yogurt /ˈyoʷgərt/ **13-12**
young /yʌŋ/ **33-15**
Yugoslavia /ˌyuʷgoʷˈslaviˠə/ **8**
Yukon Territory
/ˈyuʷkɑn ˌtɛrətɔriˠ/ **10**

Zaire /zɑˈɪər/ **8**
Zambia /ˈzæmbiˠə/ **8**
zebra /ˈziˠbrə/ **71-17**
Zimbabwe /zɪmˈbɑbwiˠ/ **8**
zip code /ˈzɪp koʷd/ **19-17**
zipper /ˈzɪpər/ **80-7**
zoo /zuʷ/ **71-A**

PHOTO CREDITS　写真提供

写真提供一覧では「ロングマン英和フォト・ディクショナリー」に写真を提供く
ださった方々をアルファベット順にご紹介しております。太字の数字は提供写
真あるいは項目が出ているページをまた括弧内の数字は写真そのものを示しま
す。

CONTRIBUTORS　協力者

以下の諸団体に対し、ご協力を深く感謝申し上げます。
特にその創造性と才能を発揮してくれた（表紙および32ページ）April Cicoro と
David Godsey の両人、また時間と労力を惜しまず忍耐強く協力していただい
たモデルの方々に、深く感謝の意を表します。

ACKNOWLEDGEMENTS 謝辞

本辞典の編集にあたっては、多くの方々からご協力をいただきましたが、特に以下の方々に謝意を表します。

☐ Carol Taylor Arley Gray — 本辞典の必要性に深い理解を示してくれたことに対して。

☐ Joanne Dresner — 編集長。忍耐力、不屈の精神、見事な決断力、そしてユーモアのセンスに対して。

☐ Penny Laporte — プロジェクト編集者。あらゆる努力と細心の配慮に対して。

☐ Joseph DePinho — その創造性に富んだデザインに対して。

☐ Stella Kupferberg — あふれんばかりのエネルギー、能力、忍耐で最上の写真を入手してくれたことに対して。

☐ Irwin Feigerbaum — 文法に関する天才的知識を提供してくれたことに対して。

☐ John Rosenthal、Ann Rosenthal、Peter Freeman — 彼らのアドバイスと協力に対して。

☐ Melody Miller（ケネディー上院議員事務所）— 親切なご指導と激励に対して。

☐ Frank Teti — ケネディー一家の見事な撮影に対して。

☐ Barbara Swarts — 傑出したヒヤリング能力に対して。

そして世界中の教師と生徒の皆様が、私たちの文化をご紹介する写真と語彙を収録した本辞典を活用して興味深く学習を進めてくださるよう願ってやみません。

Publisher: Andrew Delahunty
Editor: Lizzie Warren
Design: Dave Seabourne
                    Trevor Stanesby
Picture Research: Hilary Fletcher
Production: Clive McKeough

The Publisher and editors gratefully acknowledge the
contribution of the team who worked on the original
American English edition, particularly Joanne Dresner
and Penny Laporte.

Japanese edition revised by Haruyuki Sakamaki, Vice
President of Academics Showa Women's Institute,
Boston, MA

Longman Group UK Limited
Longman House
Burnt Mill
Harlow
Essex CM20 2JE

British Library Cataloguing in Publication Data
Rosenthal, Marilyn S. (Marilyn Silver (1940–
    Longman photo dictionary.
    1. English language. Dictionaries
    I. Title II. Freeman, Daniel B. 1920–
    423

Global edition: ISBN 0 582 07245 X (green cover)
Maruzen edition: ISBN 0 582 09486 0 (blue cover)
Maruzen edition: ISBN 4 943835 00 7

Produced by Longman Group (FE) Ltd.
Printed in Hong Kong